Escape From the Rat Race

Escape From the Rat Race

Downshifting to a Richer Life

by

Nicholas Corder

RIGHT WAY
plus

Typeset in 12/13½pt Legacy Serif Book by Letterpart Ltd., Reigate, Surrey.

Printed and bound in Great Britain by Guernsey Press Co. Ltd., Guernsey, Channel Islands.

The *Right Way Plus* series is published by Elliot Right Way Books, Brighton Road, Lower Kingswood, Tadworth, Surrey, KT20 6TD, U.K. For information about our company and the other books we publish, visit our website at www.right-way.co.uk

Contents

Acknowledgements

I am very grateful to those downshifters whose experience helped inform this book. Without them, it would have been a great deal harder to write. Without the constant help of my wife Pauline, it would have been impossible. Thank you for all your help, advice and coffee, and for reading and re-reading the various draft versions of the book.

Preface

An American tourist, on holiday in Greece, looks down from the jetty onto the beach below. A local man has just caught a couple of good-sized fish and is cooking them over an open fire, whilst he lies down, shading himself against the Mediterranean sun.

The American strikes up a conversation.

"If you caught four fish a day instead of two and sold the other two fish, eventually you'd make enough money to buy a little boat."

"What would I do with a little boat?", asked the Greek.

"Why, then you could get further away from the shore to where there are more fish. You could probably catch at least eight fish a day."

"What am I going to do with eight fish a day? I can only eat two."

"You sell the other fish. Eventually, with a bit of work, you could buy a whole fleet of little boats and employ people to go out in them and catch little fish for you."

"Why would I want to do that?"

"Just think of all the free time it could buy you."

"So what am I going to do with all this free time?"

"That's up to you. What do you like doing?"

"Actually, I like lying around on the beach eating fish."

Chapter 1:

In the Rat Race Only a Rat Can Win

The mass of men lead lives of quiet desperation

H.D.Thoreau

Does this sound anything like you?

You work long hours at a job you don't particularly like. You spend at least an hour a day commuting between home and work. On the days you go by train, it's always crowded and late. On the days you take the car, you always end up stuck in a traffic jam.

At the end of the day, you don't fancy cooking. You drink a few glasses of wine and order a take-away, trying to unwind in front of a television programme you're only watching with half an eye. You used to go to the cinema, read more, have a few hobbies. Now, even when you find you've got a bit of time, you don't seem to have the energy. With all the hours that you and your partner work, you've fallen out of the habit of doing things together. The children are more of a burden than a joy. You feel as though you are becoming increasingly alienated from your own family.

The next day, pumped up on caffeine, you go through the same thing again. Come the weekend, by the time you've done the weekly shop, mown the lawn, taken the car through the car wash, fixed the tap that's been dripping for a fortnight, caught up on the washing and ironing, dealt with a few bits of paperwork in preparation for Monday's early morning meeting, your weekend has gone. There's no escape from it at evenings and weekends, as new technology means that work can intrude into your home and family life via faxes, mobile phones and the dreaded e-mail.

You earn good money, but it never quite seems to be enough. There's always something extra to buy – for the house, for the garden, for the kids. On paper, you should have a lot, but by the time you've paid the mortgage, the car loan, the bills and so on, there's always something left on the credit card at the end of the month. Perhaps if you got that promotion, changed departments, moved to a new company, it would all be better, but . . .

You feel like you're on a hamster treadmill. You feel like you're running just to stay in the same place.

Don't you sometimes wish for something more?

Many of us feel that we are not in control of our own lives. Perhaps you would like a life where you feel that you control your work and your finances. Perhaps you would like to spend less time at work and more time with your family, otherwise, before you know it, your children will have left home and will be strangers to you.

Perhaps you'd like to pursue that hobby you always wanted to try. Maybe you fancy playing more sport, getting more exercise or watching your children in the school play.

In England, we work the longest hours of any country in the European Community. Whilst most of our continental partners knock off before they have done 40 hours, we are still at our desks, computers and lathes. The culture of working long hours is deeply ingrained. This is partly because of the economic climate. Redundancy, or perhaps more accurately the fear of redundancy through takeovers

You feel like you're on a hamster treadmill.

and mergers, the desire and need to conform to a pattern of long hours, not being seen to be the first to leave the office – all these, as well as personal choice, make for a long working week.

Of course, the work often brings with it material rewards. By working hard in a well-paid profession, you can have a nice house, a nice car, continental holidays, meals out in restaurants, smart clothes, an extensive collection of CDs and videos.

However, what happens when you've got all these

things? Are you any happier? Long working hours also bring stress, ill health and job insecurity. In fact, having a job can be an expensive way of making a living. A recent National Opinion Poll Survey revealed that 30% of respondents felt that they did not have time to deal with their own day-to-day finances. If you're not dealing with your finances, then who is?

Work is not all it is cracked up to be

Work takes up a disproportionate amount of our time – we have to travel there and we bring work home with us. It also costs us money – we have the cost of transport and clothing, just because we work.

We buy convenience foods when we feel we are too busy to cook and treat ourselves because we feel that we deserve some pampering for all our hard work. Meals out, weekends away, expensive holidays are all things that we buy in order to make it seem worthwhile doing the work. We bribe ourselves with little treats to make up for the enormous number of hours we spend at work.

In fact, we drive an entire economy based on consumer spending. We believe that the more we have, the more happiness we will find. Yet, you would be hard pushed to find any survey of a modern economy where people were happier because they owned more. It's not true. Certainly, abject poverty tends to make people miserable. On the other hand, once you have fulfilled your basic needs for warmth, housing, food and kicked in a few minor luxuries, having anything more does not make you any happier. We tend to think that if we own a newer car, a more intelligent dishwasher or a more powerful computer we will all feel better about ourselves. Who are we kidding? In fact, sometimes it has the opposite effect as we go into debt to buy the objects of our desires.

And this is another wonder. You would expect that with our high incomes, we would have loads more money. Since the last war, incomes have at least doubled in real terms, yet we have large debts and comparatively few savings. The continual bombardment of advertising tells us what we should drink, eat, smoke, cook or smear on our faces and under our arms. We are urged to buy certain brands that will make us more stylish, cool, romantic, desirable, happy, attractive, slim, fast, witty – all-round much better people. We will even buy clothes and sports bags that do nothing more than carry enormous advertising names, logos and slogans for the manufacturers.

So, we are all encouraged to have lifestyles that we assume everyone else wants. We may think we are too sophisticated to be taken in by advertising or 'keeping up with the Joneses', but we all do it to some extent or other.

The truth is that, unless we are very hollow indeed, we should not be lured by brand names. Consumer reports and tests frequently show that the quality of designer-label goods is no better and often worse than less prestigious labels that are often far less expensive. Yet we continue to buy them.

The effect we have on the environment is telling. All these consumer goods come in their own packaging. Each week, we dispose of thousands of tonnes of rubbish, much of which could be recycled. More importantly, much of it was entirely unnecessary in the first place. I ask you – just how much cardboard, cellophane and pins does a new shirt really need?

It would seem that the more we earn, the less we have. We live in one of the wealthiest countries in the world at a time of the greatest affluence and comfort that mankind has ever known, but some of us are as miserable as sin.

If any of this strikes a chord with you, perhaps it is time that you considered downshifting.

What is downshifting?

Downshifting is about simplifying your life to make you stop thinking of your work as being the centre of your life. It is a means of controlling your life and living it on your own terms, rather than somebody else's. It is a means of balancing your life to give yourself not just financial security, but emotional security as well.

The Americans sometimes call downshifting "voluntary simplicity". This is a good way of putting it. It is voluntary, so you do it out of choice. We are also talking about simplicity and not poverty. Poverty is unpleasant, grinding and degrading. It also carries with it the stigma that you are incapable of looking after yourself. Simplicity is not the same as poverty. It is about realising that many of the trappings of a material existence are not worth the effort involved in obtaining them.

Downshifting is about realising that there is more to life than chasing material goods and that we need to balance our work with hobbies, sports, the family, voluntary work and real free time.

It's not a new idea. Jesus was a downshifter, so was Mohammed. In the nineteenth century the American author and philosopher Henry Thoreau took himself off to live in a log cabin for several years. More recently, Ghandi lived a simple life.

In England, perhaps the best known downshifters were Tom and Barbara Good, in the 1970s television series *The Good Life*. They swapped the life of the office for that of self-sufficiency. *The Good Life* was a sitcom and consequently exaggerated both the life of the Goods, struggling but determined in their alternative existence, and also the Leadbetters, Jerry and Margo, who lived a life of luxury in comparison.

Downshifting doesn't have to be about converting your

garden into a smallholding, nor does it have to be about keeping chickens or a return to the land – although it can be if you want. It is not about giving up luxuries. Electricity, central heating, television, CDs – the trappings of modern life – can be incorporated into a downshifter's life, but they take on a different meaning.

Many people have already done it, so why not you? But . . . But . . . But . . .

Downshifting is just for the rich

You might also think that downshifting is only for people who are at least reasonably well-off, if not downright rich. To an extent this is true. A large number of downshifters are people who have taken early retirement from good jobs and are supplementing a pension with part-time work. The more money you have, the easier it is to downshift. However, everything is relative. If you are used to budgeting more tightly than someone who is better off, then this is a skill you can bring to bear on your downshifting.

So what am I going to do for money?

For a start, you're not going to worry too much about it. However, unless you organise both your existing finances and your income for when you do downshift, you will not be able to do it and will end up "upshifting" again. This book is not about condemning you to a life of soulless poverty, and throughout it there are ideas for planning your finances, making your money work for you, and how to go about discovering what you really want to do in order to earn money.

I actually quite like my job, it's just the hours I put in

Be brave. Tell your boss that you want more time with the family. Get all your co-workers to agree that on one evening a week, you should all go home no later than at the official end to the working day. You can easily incorporate certain downshifting ideas into your daily life, without going the whole hog and growing root vegetables on a smallholding thirty-three miles from the nearest electric socket. It will make your life richer, simpler and more pleasant.

What about my career?

You can still have a career. It's just it won't be the kind of career where you move up the ladder rung by rung. If you downshift, it means abandoning a traditional pattern of work for one that means that you do not have this vertical path. There may be no way back for you if you decide that downshifting is not for you and want to return to your former career at a later stage. This is an important decision so don't rush into it. It needs discussing with family and friends.

Most middle-class people are caught up in the idea of having a career. Very often what they mean by this is a vertical career that has them climbing that ladder in some organisation or other. Fine. If that's what you want to do, I'm not going to stop you from getting on with it. Some people like the challenge, kudos and rewards that come with this. Many of us don't. In fact, I suspect that there is a large number of silent sufferers who feel that they are simply stuck on a treadmill and want to get off. Some of us just find the whole ladder fatuous, silly and a complete waste of time.

However, don't forget that if you do give up your career, you will no longer be able to define yourself by the job you do.

Some of us just find the ladder fatuous . . .

What will I do if I give up my job?

Downshifting does not necessarily mean giving up your job. It might mean changing jobs; for instance, finding the same kind of work, but closer to home so you can walk rather than drive. It might mean finding a new way of working, such as telecommuting. It might mean working part-time, rather than full-time, or becoming self-employed. You could even stay in your current job, but adopt some of the attitudes of a downshifter, as I have already suggested.

If you are going to downshift, your attitude to work is one of the most important things you will have to change.

I can't downshift just yet

No, perhaps you can't, but you can at least be thinking about it. Successful downshifters are people who have got their act together. They have decided what they want from life and set out to get it. You can start making plans, toying with ideas and discussing what you are going to do in the future, so that when the time comes to make the change, you're ready.

But I still can't do it until I've paid off my mortgage

Fair enough. So why not make plans to pay off your mortgage more quickly? Sensible financial planning is at the heart of downshifting. Re-evaluating the way you spend your money is an essential part of the process. The best time to start planning is now.

I like owning nice things

If you are driven by financial and material success, you may not enjoy giving it all up. If happiness is owning the smartest car on the block, you are not going to feel buoyed up by the thought of knocking around in a second-hand car. If you like where you live so much that you could never leave your house, but you have a large mortgage, it is going to be very difficult for you to downshift. Perhaps it is something you would need to consider at a later stage, once you have worked out your finances a little more.

Downshifting does not mean having to give up owning nice things. Many downshifters do not go without all the frills – they just don't get driven by them.

You have to accept that downshifting is not for everybody.

How can I put my family through this?

First of all, any big life change like downshifting needs to be discussed with all the members of the family. Downshifting is bound to have a huge effect on your lifestyle, aspirations and general philosophy. Teenage children can be especially fond of the material things in life. It is a big step and one not to be taken lightly.

On the other hand, how can you put your family through what you're doing at the moment? Working crazy hours, choosing work commitments over family ones, changing holiday plans at the last moment because of these commitments and seeing your family far less than you would like. Perhaps they might actually like you to change.

What will other people think about me?

Talk to friends who you think might understand your proposed new way of life, as well as to those you think will only point out the pitfalls. You might find that many of them will be very sympathetic towards your ideas. And anyway, even if they aren't, does it really matter? One of the great joys of downshifting is *not* keeping up with the Joneses. Do you really care what the Joneses think?

Don't you have to be an environmentalist vegetarian communist to downshift?

No. Downshifting is concerned with safeguarding the environment, but it also accepts that we are living in a modern, technological world. That's why we call it "downshifting" rather than "dropping out". So, for instance, it's perfectly legitimate to be a downshifter and still own a motor car. And why not? It's a great form of transport. However, a downshifter might use a bicycle before public transport and public transport before their own car, but it does not mean that they wouldn't necessarily use a car. After all, we are living in the real world.

If downshifters do tend towards vegetarianism, it is largely for financial reasons. Vegetables and pulses are cheaper than meat.

I suspect (but I don't know for sure) that many downshifters may be left-leaning or liberal in their politics, but you are allowed to downshift whatever your politics and *The Times* is cheaper than *The Guardian*.

So what's it like as a downshifter?

Often friends look at our lifestyle and say, "It's all right for you, you don't have to wear a tie/go to the dry cleaners/dress smartly/impress the boss/keep a house like this running", and so on.

In fact, I do have to do all those things, although not nearly as much or as often as they do. I have balanced work with the rest of my life. I spend a great deal of my time working, but not always for money. However, more and more I am learning to streamline the work that I do, so that I am working at what interests me and not what other people want me to do.

Downshifting is a question of degree. There is no absolute in downshifting. In the next chapter, you will meet my imaginary commuter, Paul, who brings home £20,000 per annum. To some people, living on £20,000 a year would seem like downshifting, to others it may look like a King's Ransom. It's about three times as much as you would get if you were earning the national minimum wage.

If your idea of downshifting is living in a log cabin, eating the fruits of the forest and communing deeply with nature, then that's great – go for it.

On the other hand, if brewing your own wine instead of

drinking Chateau Rothschild, hanging on to your car for five years rather than the usual two, and taking a foreign holiday only on alternate years, seems like downshifting to you, then that's exactly what it is.

Jealousy should not be a part of downshifting. If you start saying, "Well, I could downshift if I was on £50,000 a year/ had a company car/knew I was going to inherit a Georgian mansion," you won't ever get round to downshifting at all.

So when can I start?

You can downshift just as soon as you've decided that it's right for you. But remember – there's always a cost in delay.

Chapter 2:

Money is Time

I have long been of the opinion that if work were such a splendid thing the rich would have kept more of it for themselves.

Bruce Grocott

The idea of fixed time is a relatively new one. It was 'invented' by the railway companies in the nineteenth century. Before then, "time" was a fairly flexible idea. Sure, they divided the time into hours, minutes and seconds just as we do today, but twelve mid-day in London might be half-past twelve in Manchester and twenty to twelve in Birmingham. People would arrange to meet in the afternoon, or in the morning – there was no great need to be any more precise than that. Many clocks did not have a minute hand. Pocket or wrist watches were a rarity. Even clocks in houses were the preserve of the wealthy few. The clock on the nearest church tower provided the time for most of the local population.

With the arrival of the railways came the need to standardise times, so that we knew when a train was going to arrive or depart and that time meant the same thing to everyone at every station along the line.

Nowadays, you can have a watch that is linked electronically to a signal from Greenwich, which means that the time on your wrist is always exact to the nearest nanosecond. The idea of seeing someone "tomorrow afternoon" is a luxury.

We want to be precise. Unpunctuality is rude and wastes our time.

Of course, the division of time into segments of hours, minutes, seconds and so on is a false one. The idea that a working day lasts a set number of hours is a hangover from the Industrial Revolution. Another is the introduction of good quality artificial light, which means that we can work at any time of the day or night because we can now see what we are doing. Artificial light, and the false working day that results, means that we have lost our natural rhythms of work, sleep and leisure. There is a fundamental problem with our body clocks.

In addition, we are pressurised by the idea that time equals money. The boss is always telling us that time is money. When we pay our garage repair bill, we are charged a labour cost based on an hourly rate. When we sit in traffic jams, we could be winning another sale, writing another report or doing something else that will bring in money. If we sell a service, we usually sell it on the basis of the amount of time it takes us to do the job.

But time is not money. It is not like money. There is a fundamental difference between the two. If I give you a hundred pounds at the beginning of the day, you can spend it or save it. If you save it, when you wake up tomorrow morning, you will still have a hundred pounds. If you invest it, you may have even more.

Time is not the same. You cannot "save" time. You cannot suddenly decide to save all the hours of today and use them tomorrow. When you wake up tomorrow morning, today will be gone. You won't get to re-use the time you had today. Once time has gone, it has gone. This means that it is really important to use time in the best way you possibly can.

Going to work is not necessarily the best use you could make of your time.

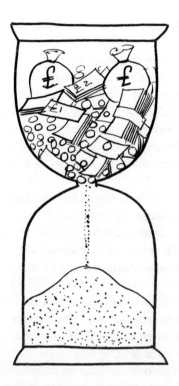

We are pressurised by the idea that time equals money.

Let's crunch some numbers

In this country, the average man, if he is lucky enough to have a job, puts in a forty-four hour week. In London, the average is nearer fifty hours per week. Ten percent of the workforce work for 48 hours a week or more, which is above the Working Times Regulation threshold. In other words, around 2.7 million workers are putting in this sort of time. Four percent work for 60 or more hours per week.

Sometimes, working longer hours is by choice. Often, hourly-paid workers have a chance to earn overtime payments by working additional hours. Very few workers are, in fact, forced to work long hours. A survey by the Institute of Personnel Development found that 41% of those working more than 48 hours a week did so because they believed it was the only way in which to get the work done. They may not be forced, but they don't seem to have a choice – a nice distinction if ever there was one. There is a danger that working long hours has become part of the culture of many offices. At the moment, our work culture makes a virtue of workaholism.

Apart from hourly paid workers looking to supplement their incomes, most of those working a long week are professional or managerial workers, but the tendency is creeping into all levels of our organisations. According to the magazine *Business Page*, 85% of PAs and secretaries regularly work beyond their contracted hours. Only a third of these get any kind of overtime payment.

The unspoken reason why so many of us work these kinds of hours is that, if we are busy, we must be important. Busyness is a kind of status symbol. Displaying to others in the workplace that one is constantly on the go assures us of a good reputation amongst co-workers and managers.

There is more to work than simply the hours we put in at the office. Work spills out beyond the office walls. Nearly seventy percent of professional workers take work home with them in the evenings.

There is also work-related time to take into account. By this, I mean the time that we spend on activities that are not work itself, but which are related to work, such as commuting, buying clothes for work, preparing to go to work, indulging in work-related social activities that we might choose not to attend under other circumstances.

Commuting is often the largest of the additional time factors. The average Londoner who commutes by car spends eighty-two minutes every day behind the wheel. This adds up to nearly seven hours every week. According to Eurostat, the statistical branch of the European Union, this time excludes "exceptional" jams. Some days, that eighty-two minutes will stretch out just that little bit more.

So, let's work through an example. Let's take an imaginary fellow called Paul and base him in London. We will give him a reasonably generous net income of £20,000 after he has paid out tax, National Insurance and pension contributions. He is contracted to work a 37½ hour week and gets six weeks annual leave, including public holidays.

To work out his hourly net rate of pay, we simply have to divide the amount he earns (£20,000) by his annual hours (46 × 37.5 = 1725). This would give Paul an hourly pay rate of about £11.60. However, we need to take other factors into account.

Paul is an average sort of chap, so he works an average forty-four hour week. We'll also say that when it comes to commuting, Paul spends the average length of time of seven hours a week travelling between home and work. Although he owns a car, he travels to work by public transport. He also spends an hour every other week shopping for clothes and other bits and pieces for work. He also goes to the pub with colleagues on Friday lunch-time, the only day of the week when he does take a proper lunch break, although this is out of habit rather than a genuine desire to spend time with his co-workers.

Now, most people would think that Paul would be reasonably comfortably off and was earning a fairly decent wage. It's not a fortune, by any stretch of the imagination, but it is far from Skid Row.

So what does that mean that Paul earns as an hourly rate?

Work	46 weeks @ 44 hours per week =	2024
Commuting	46 weeks @ 7 hours per week =	322

Work-related shopping	23 weeks @ 1 hour per week =	23
Pub-time	46 weeks @ 1 hour per week =	46
Total time spent on work and work-related activities =		**2415**

So, Paul can say that, netting £20,000 for 2415 hours of work-related time, he is on a real hourly rate of £8.28.

Work-related expenditure

Now, that still doesn't seem too bad – it's over double the minimum wage. There are millions of people in this country who would think that this is really good money. But this is still not the whole picture. What we've not taken into account is any of the expenditure Paul has through being at work.

Paul has transport costs. In his office, he is expected to dress reasonably smartly and so has to own several suits or jackets and trousers, ties, shoes and so forth.

As he works such long hours and spends so much time commuting he finds that he needs a little help around the house. He has a cleaner two mornings a week, who also does his ironing. He buys takeaways at least twice a week, because it saves him the bother of cooking. He also shares in the cost of hiring help to undertake gardening, window-cleaning and low-level maintenance chores – things that, had he the time, he would probably do himself. If he had children, he might also have the additional costs of crèche fees and baby-sitting to look after them whilst he is at work.

There are also hidden costs if working the hours that you do means that you have to undertake your leisure activities – the gym, the cinema, the theatre, holidays – at peak times, when they tend to cost more.

Transport costs are difficult to calculate, especially if you use your own car. You already own the car, so there are certain fixed costs that you are going to have to pay anyway, such as road tax, insurance and membership of a breakdown organisation. Then there are the variable costs, largely based on how many miles you drive, which include fuel, repairs and so on.

In Paul's case, he buys a season ticket, which costs him £2,000 per annum. In addition, he reckons that he spends £500 a year on clothes for work. His Friday lunches cost him £10 per week. His cleaning and ironing run to £20 per week, gardening and so forth another £20, and he spends a further £15 a week on takeaway meals when he feels particularly tired.

Season ticket =		£2,000
Lunches =	46 × £10 =	£460
Cleaning and Ironing =	52 × £20 =	£1040
Gardening, etc. =	52 × £20 =	£1040
Takeaways =	52 × £15 =	£780
Total =		£5,320

If we now deduct the £5,320 of work-related expenditure from his net income of £20,000 per annum, we can say that a more realistic net income is £14,680. If we then recalculate his hourly rate, taking this into account, we can see that it works out at £6.08.

But there are other indirect costs

Even when we have calculated this figure, we still have not taken into account many of the luxuries in which Paul indulges himself, purely to help him relax from the stresses of the job.

He finds that the pressure of work means that he likes to

go to the gym to unwind. This costs him £500 per year. Short breaks away from London are a life-saver; without them he would go mad. Three of these each year cost Paul £900. He also treats himself to one really good holiday every year so as to really get away from it all and this normally costs him £1,500, sometimes even more. He also treats himself to the odd CD, a bottle of expensive wine or a video, just so as to perk himself up, especially if he has had a bad week at work. These amount to about £20 a week or £1,000 a year.

Gym =	£500
Short breaks =	£900
Luxury Holiday =	£1,500
"Treats" =	£1,000
Total =	**£3,900**

If we then recalculate Paul's hourly rate, we can then say that the original £20,000 is reduced by £5,320 for direct costs, and by a further £3,900 for the luxuries that help him get through his working year. This means that his original £20,000 is now reduced to just £10,780 or an hourly rate of £4.46. This is a long way from our initial idea that he earns £11.60 per hour.

And Paul is "only" working a forty-four hour week. If Paul started to work the fifty hours a week that Eurostat suggests the average Londoner works, his hourly rate would be a meagre £4.01. If he's one of the 33% of workers who don't take their full holiday entitlement, then his rate probably drops even lower.

Again, there are many people who would think that this is good money, but don't forget that we started out saying that Paul earns £20,000 after tax, and we reckon that almost half his net income goes on maintaining him in his job.

If Paul were a family man, his position might be even worse. According to a National Opinion Poll survey undertaken on behalf of Abbey National, 72% of families buy takeaways each week because they don't have the time to prepare food for themselves. Another estimate reckons that many ordinary families are parting with as much as £5,000 every year on the kind of everyday tasks that people once did for themselves, such as ironing, cleaning, housework and cooking. We're all having to work so hard that we have to spend more and more money just to keep our households running smoothly.

Frighteningly, according to the charity the Daycare Trust, a family with one school-age child and another under the age of 5 will spend £6,000 per year on childcare expenditure. If one parent is working purely to be able to afford childcare provision and the costs of buying in "household maintenance", then there is room for some serious re-thinking about the whole point of being a double income family.

On the other hand, sometimes we protest just a little bit too much and part with this kind of money just so that we can slump in front of our television sets. We spend an average of 25 hours a week watching the goggle box and then we all rush out to buy exercise bicycles in order to put right the lack of physical fitness that results from our lives as couch potatoes.

More to work than money

So far, we have only looked at work in terms of the financial costs. There are other costs as well. There are social costs, emotional costs and physical costs, as well as there being stresses and strains on both you and your family. There are even stresses to the organisations themselves as workers make mistakes when tired and often others find themselves working additional hours to put right work that has not been done properly in the first place.

There are two main types of long hours workers. There are the 'workafrolics' and the 'workaholics'. Workafrolics love their work so much that they would rather be working than anything else. Workaholics, on the other hand, feel driven to work long and hard, but do not get any real enjoyment from doing it.

There's probably little wrong in being a Workafrolic. Deriving fun from doing something is good for you. If you work long hours because you love your work, it is unlikely to do you any harm. You probably see any new pressure or difficulty at work as a new challenge, which you can meet with relish.

What if you belong to the second group? If you are working long hours for the sake of it, rather than because you enjoy what you are doing, you are open to a range of illnesses. The kinds of situations on which your workafrolic colleagues thrive could be very dangerous to you. You are addicted to work not because you enjoy it, but because you are driven to do so. You are much more likely to suffer from stress, general health problems and disturbed sleeping patterns than your workafrolic mate. Losing sleep lowers the response of your immune system and makes you more vulnerable to a range of other illnesses.

It's not just your health that is at stake. In a workaholic culture, there are also dangers to your relationships with your family, spouse, partner or children. You may neglect your friends and any leisure activities. Workaholism means constantly living in an atmosphere of unnecessary pressure.

Sometimes you might think that you're the only person in the world who feels this way. I can assure you that you are not. According to the Institute of Personnel Development, almost half of all workers think that they dedicate too much of their lives to their work. Over half of the people in their survey resented working the longer hours to some extent or other, even if they did so "voluntarily".

The stress on relationships can be enormous. The same report also points out that 11% of younger workers had split up with a partner over the last few years because of the pressure of work. Three per cent of people in their survey reckoned that their marriages had ended as a result of overwork. It would be almost impossible to calculate to what extent working too many hours has been a contributing factor to relationships faltering, flickering or dying.

Furthermore, according to Diane Fassel, an organisational consultant, workaholics are "dishonest, controlling, judgmental, perfectionist, self-centred, dualistic in their thinking, confused, crisis oriented, and ultimately spiritually bankrupt."

Now, if that's beginning to sound something like you, don't you think it's time you did something about it?

Being too busy for activities other than work is also spiritually very dangerous. It can stifle your creativity and means that you are missing out on the world around you. You've seen the tourist who is constantly busy with his video camera all the time. He misses the bigger picture by concentrating only on what he can see through his viewfinder. The same is true of work. Centre your life around work and you too can miss out on the wider vistas of life.

There's no doubt that the pace of working life has increased over the past few years. In fact, a survey by Cambridge University showed that over 60% of employees claim that the pace of work has increased since 1990. They also re-assert that there is a definite link between job insecurity and the intensification of work, and such unpleasant side effects as poor health and tense family relationships.

When it boils down to it, you can't really "save time", but you can decide how you are going to spend it.

Now, if you are beginning to think that you are one of

Diane Fassel's workaholics or you are living, as are so many people, with the threat of insecurity over your job, then maybe you should start re-thinking your life. After all, in the few short years between 1992 and 1995 one quarter of all home-owning households of working age suffered from a loss of a job and/or income.

It might be better to organise your own parachute before they throw you out of the aeroplane without one.

Chapter 3:

Shopping – Why More Means Less

We used to build civilisations. Now we build shopping malls.

Bill Bryson

The pressure is on us to buy. No matter how much we might try to resist, most of us end up buying far more things than we ever intend to. The result is that our wardrobes bulge with clothes we never wear, our larders and fridges fill up with food that will only rot and we buy books which we can't stomach beyond the first page.

You have the best of intentions. You go to the supermarket with a list of exactly what you want. You're not going to buy anything that's not on the list. But that three-for-the-price-of-two offer on fresh cream cakes was just too hard to resist, and when you saw the smart, stainless steel serving spoons, you thought how tatty the old ones looked; and besides, at those prices, they were almost giving them away.

Even if you make the most comprehensive shopping list and vow to stick to it religiously, it's very hard not to end up coming home with something you never intended buying.

We know we're letting ourselves down, so why do we do it?

What makes us buy things is a complicated business. Sure, there are things that we have to get in order to eat, keep warm or feed our imaginations, but once we have satisfied those basic human needs, we still seem to go on shopping. It's not surprising that we spend so much money:

we're surrounded by pressure, temptation and role models of people far wealthier than we will ever be.

Wise up to the advertisers

We're not stupid. We all know we are surrounded by advertising. We are all intelligent enough to realise that we are being constantly bombarded with images of what we are told we need to own in order to make our lives better.

This is especially true for those of us who have a television set. If you watch the commercial channels, you only get fifteen or twenty minutes of real programming before you are interrupted by a stream of adverts telling you how to have shinier hair, a cleaner kitchen, a smarter car, a trimmer waist-line, quicker pizza or a more flexible credit card. On the rare occasions, such as a football match, when they can't get their fifteen minute fixes, they stuff the half-time interval full of adverts. We even have individual sponsorship of programmes, so we can link chocolate or washing powder with our favourite soap opera, financial institutions with dramas, beer with our detectives.

If we escape from the cocoon of our living rooms and go to the cinema, not only do we have to sit through more direct advertisements, but we have to suffer the indirect ones during the film itself. Spot a well-known brand of cola or beer or cigarettes in a film and the likelihood is that it is a case of "product placement". Canny film producers employ people to look through film scripts to spot exactly where they might be able to place certain products. If the script reads, "She takes a can of cat food from the fridge", they will try to get makers of pet food to pay them to put their brand in the heroine's fridge. When the hero climbs out of his car, pops the ring on his beer can, opens a packet of cigarettes, slips on his sun-glasses as he eyes the heroine in her slinky evening dress, it's a fair assumption that every one of those products has brought the film producers money.

The forces which work to make you spend your money are even subtler than most of us realise.

How shops make you buy stuff

Shops exist in order to get us to spend money in them. The large chains of shops spend a fortune researching the best ways for you to part with your hard-earned cash. They are very clever indeed at doing this.

Every aspect of a shop is thought out thoroughly. Its layout, the atmosphere it wants to create and the image it wants to give its customers have all been studied and considered with the utmost care.

Take your humble local sub-post office. I suspect yours is pretty much like thousands of others throughout the country. As well as dealing with post office business such as stamps, pensions, various forms and so forth, it probably also sells other things as well – perhaps sweets, newspapers, cigarettes or general groceries. Where is the actual post office counter section of the shop? I can almost guarantee you that it will be at the back of the shop. You may think this is for security reasons – sub-post offices do get held up by robbers from time to time. A more likely explanation is that it forces you to walk through the display area of the shop to get to the post office area at the back. You might just stop and buy something else on the way.

Now, I'm not saying this in order to have a go at sub-post offices, which are worthy of our support, but to show you how they think. These are small shops. Imagine how the large stores, who want so much more of our money, plan their layouts.

As you move through the store, you will be following a pattern that the retailer has carefully devised and which he monitors at all times, surrounded by well-researched colour schemes which invite you unwittingly to buy.

Supermarkets, for instance, often follow a grid pattern, where you move up and down the aisles. You may not think it when you pick up a packet of broken biscuits, but everything on the supermarket's shelves has been placed there with the utmost care. The people who design supermarkets are incredibly clever. They have done a vast amount of research into the way people move around the supermarkets, looking for goods. They know exactly the best position within the store for tins of baked beans, fresh produce, boxes of chocolates or frozen meats.

Next time you're in the supermarket, just try this little experiment. Notice how all the basic foodstuffs that you want, that you buy week in and week out, are at inconvenient heights. You will probably realise that anything that is displayed at eye level is there to catch your eye. Also notice the way in which the ends of each aisle, what they call the "hot spots", are stacked with special, tempting displays to drag you in.

Sometimes, when you go to your local supermarket, you find they've moved the baked beans. If you accuse them of being stupid or inconsistent or inconsiderate, I'm afraid you're wrong. The reason they have moved those beans is to make you look for them. Whilst looking for them, you will find other things that you might be tempted to buy along the way.

Clustering all the ingredients that you might use to make a curry around one particular display stand is not the supermarket being helpful, but their attempt to make sure that you buy a whole load of other things that you might just have opted to go without.

Just think about it when you go shopping. Instead of asking yourself the question, "What am I going to buy?", ask yourself, "What is this shop doing to try to make me buy things?". The other day, for instance, I found myself in a well-known high street retailer that sells food and clothing. The food hall was at the back of the shop and, in order to get to it, I had to pass through the menswear department. Now, I know that some men like going shopping, but I suspect that there are several million of us who don't. I would bet that the reason why you had to go through menswear was to force you to browse areas that you would not normally look at.

Don't make the mistake of thinking that loyalty cards exist in order to "reward" you for your custom. They exist purely in order to hook you into continuing to spend money in a particular shop. The crèche, the baby changing facilities, the cash machines, the café, the bag packing service are not there out of the kindness of the supermarkets' hearts: they are facilities to draw you in to the shop.

There are also far more ways to shop than ever before. You've got your little specialist shops, supermarkets, hyper-markets and shopping malls. You can go to retail parks, out-of-town stores or factory outlets. Town centres are pedestrianised so you can wander more easily between the shops. You can buy mail order, over the telephone or using the Internet. The whole concept of "consumer choice" seems to be that people who sell things must have the right to be able to sell them twenty-four hours a day for three hundred and sixty-five days of the year, using whatever means possible. It's not really "consumer choice" at all; it's retailers' rights.

How the shops always win

The big shops know more about us than you would ever care to imagine. They know why people go shopping. The little plastic card that you use to rack up points in the supermarket gives them huge amounts of data about us as individual shoppers and helps them to stock and manage their stores appropriately.

On top of this, they use university-level research to work out what motivates us to go to the shops in the first place and why we buy what we do when we get there. We don't go shopping just to buy stuff. We go because we are expected to, as a diversion from work, as an antidote to boredom or loneliness, as a means of alleviating depression, to learn about new trends and ideas, to get a bit of exercise or to fill our senses with the colours, sights and sounds of the big shops.

We might find that we like meeting up with people, or simply watching them going about their own shopping. We might like to hang around a particular hobby shop to meet with like-minded enthusiasts. We could simply be doing a little bit of showing off by dressing our best and parading round the shopping mall. We might get a thrill from the levels of service offered by the more select shops or simply enjoy a little bit of a haggle or the thought that we are getting a bargain.

There is no doubt that recreational shopping has become ingrained in what we do. In the week in which I am writing this, there is a weekday television show that comes from a shopping mall, which seems to do little but encourage people to spend money.

How the goods trick you

We can all see how quickly technology is changing. I am writing this on a computer that fits on my desktop. It has more power than a room-sized computer would have had a generation ago. Buy a television today and it will be old technology within six months.

If you do buy something with the intention of keeping it for years, you run the risk of buying something that also has "built-in obsolescence". The parts of your machine, or whatever, are deliberately manufactured to a standard that is only high enough to give the equipment a certain length of life.

In order to lull us into thinking that our electronic goods are going to give us years of trouble-free service, shops also try to sell us special insurance that will enable us to have our white goods repaired free of charge. Of course, the insurance is very expensive and they are making a huge profit on it, but it gives us peace of mind, so many of us buy it.

And then, fashions change. Your chrome kettle, which still works perfectly well, now begins to look old hat.

Nowhere can the shifts in fashion be seen more obviously than in clothing. Each season brings with it a new "in" colour. Keep up with trends in clothing and you'll soon fill your wardrobe with clothes that are unwearable, simply because they look dated.

Whilst fashion has its seasons, the fresh produce, which used to be available only when in season, is now available all year round. Tangerines used to be a Christmas treat; strawberries were for the summer. More sophisticated growing techniques and international trade mean that we can have these things all year round – at a price.

And there is also so much more to buy. My local supermarket is not a particularly big one, but it boasts twelve different types of cat food and five sorts of baked beans. There are fruits and vegetables that were unheard of a generation ago.

It's no wonder, with all this pressure, that we end up buying far more than we ever need.

The Joneses have got one

The idea of keeping up with the Joneses was that you saw what your next-door neighbour had got and decided that you had to have one too. Mr. Jones bought a new lawn mower, so did you. Mr. Jones went on holiday to Torremolinos, so did

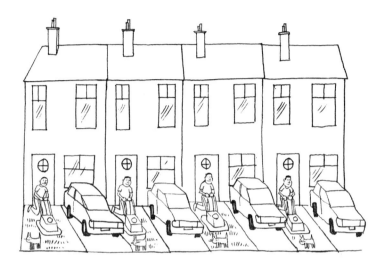

The Joneses have got one . . .

you. Mr. Jones bought a fondue set, so did you.

Mr. Jones, living next door to you, probably lives in a fairly similar house to yours, he possibly earns a similar amount of money to you. The problem is that films and television have enabled us to look into places that are far plusher than Mr. Jones' house.

We are conned into believing that everyone has more money than we do and that the money brings with it happiness, a more attractive partner, more respect, greater freedom – in short that the richer we are, the better we are.

We're all customers now

It doesn't stop at the adverts, though. Turning to the television guide for the week in which I am writing this chapter, I can see that shopping is an important part of the schedules. On terrestrial television, there are at least eleven programmes devoted to shopping – several of these are repeated in the same week. On top of that, there are also programmes about re-decorating your house, collecting antiques or making over your garden. These programmes aren't about shopping, but they do have at the heart of them either a need for money to do the work or downright greed as you ransack granny's attic for stuff that might be worth a few bob.

On satellite television, there are even entire channels that are devoted to shopping. These have programmes that are essentially a series of advertisements for various products and you can telephone with your credit card to snap up the latest in plastic gimmickry.

We have television shows based around the National Lottery. We have quiz shows offering million pound prizes. We can win trips around the world or television sets by potting snooker balls. We can win hi-fi systems by knowing the simplest of proverbs or the capital city of France. And when we relax away from quiz shows and watch dramas or comedy programmes, we are often catapulted into the lives of people who seem to be far better off materially than we are.

It's not just television either. You can't escape it. From the company logos on the football strip to the Formula One driver's multi-badged suit, we're surrounded by the pressure to buy and consume from billboards, magazines, newspapers and films.

Through our doors every day come invitations to enter prize draws, to do the football pools, change our windows for gleaming new plastic ones, take out a loan, and get our take-aways from the new shop in the High Street. We are absolutely bombarded with the stuff.

We're all customers now. A few years ago, you could go into hospital safe in the knowledge that you would be a patient. Now you're a customer. You can't travel by rail as a passenger anymore; you're a customer. Clubs no longer have members; they have customers. Everybody wants our custom.

In other words, our importance to most large organisations is not as human beings, but as consumers of whatever it is they want us to consume.

I suspect that most of us know this already. After all, we're not stupid. But it wears you down and all of us succumb in our different ways.

What are we trying to buy?

Today's generation has far more money than any previous generations. We are probably twice as well-off as our parents. Compared with our ancestors of only a hundred years ago, we have far more material wealth and far more possessions.

Take a look around your house. It is highly likely to contain a television set, a video recorder, a hi-fi system, several radios, comfortable seating and all sorts of kitchen equipment – a fridge, washing machine, dish-washer, tumble-dryer, cooker, electric kettle, toaster and microwave. Look in your bedroom drawers and cupboards and you will probably find five, ten, possibly even twenty times as many clothes as your ancestors of 1900, who would have been considered very wealthy if they had had more than three changes of clothes. Your house may also very well be centrally heated, double-glazed and fully carpeted throughout. We are living in an age of great material wealth and comfort.

And why shouldn't we? After all, our ancestors didn't have a lot of the things that we have because they were either not invented or had not yet been made widely available.

I am not suggesting for a moment that we should go without these kinds of things, either. If you are downshifting, you don't have to give up these material advantages.

What you do have to do, however, is re-think your relationship with material goods.

Let me put it another way. Central heating makes our lives much more comfortable. There is little reason why you should be uncomfortable by not heating your home. You should enjoy the material comforts that modern living has to offer.

The question you really should be asking yourself is, "How much do I really need?"

We are what we buy

We now place such an importance on having possessions that shopping has become the nation's favourite leisure activity. Every weekend the shopping malls and department stores of Britain heave with huge numbers of shoppers, picking over mounds of clothing, electrical goods, the latest in films, music, fashion, make-up and gizmos.

Many of these shoppers are not actually looking for anything in particular. They are entirely happy to browse, eventually making a series of impulse buys. At the end of a long Saturday spent trudging round overheated stores, they will have consumed huge quantities of fast food and have armfuls of carrier bags, each emblazoned with the name of the shop. Yes, even the logos on the carrier bags count in a world that has become increasingly consumerist.

You hear people joking about doing this kind of shopping. They don't equate it with going to the supermarket to get the weekly grocery shop. No, this is entirely different. Going to the supermarket is a chore. Going to the out-of-town mall or shopping centre is all part of shopping for fun. People even call it "retail therapy". True, there is a bit of self-deprecating British irony in all this, but it does contain the idea that after you've spent all week working hard to earn your money, you deserve a treat. So now that you've got a little bit of time at the weekend, you should pamper yourself by spending some of that hard-earned money on a few objects of desire to help you through the week.

In fact, it's not therapy at all, but the road to being less and less in charge of your life. The simple truth is that owning stuff is an expensive business. Nearly everything that you buy carries with it an additional expense.

Let's imagine that you do not watch a lot of television, although you do own a television set. Up until now, you have resisted the temptation to buy a video recorder. They are now extremely cheap and affordable. There's nothing wrong with buying a VCR. It's an inexpensive form of entertainment and it allows you to be discriminate in your viewing habits. You decide to buy one.

However, it's not enough just to buy a video recorder. Once you've bought one, you also need to buy video cassettes so you can record programmes, otherwise it's rather pointless. This is an additional expense caused entirely by owning a VCR. This much is fairly obvious.

Then your television breaks down. Before you owned the video, you might have said, "Ah well, I don't watch a lot of TV, maybe I'll just get by without one." However, now you have more money invested in your television set-up. Without a TV set, you can't watch the videos you have recorded and your investment in a video recorder is going to waste. You must now do something about your television set. And televisions are pretty cheap nowadays, so instead of wasting money by having it repaired (because it might break down again), you may as well buy a new set.

Growing used to having the VCR, you also start buying and renting films to watch. The trouble is that you enjoy the films so much that you start thinking how nice it would be to have a new DVD player, so you end up buying one of those as well. Now that you can get a much better quality of sound and picture, it's time to upgrade your telly again, and so on.

We all know the person who buys the latest hi-fi system. As soon as he carries it out of the shop, it is old technology. He can never catch up on himself. Whatever he owns will soon be superseded by the latest model. And does it make him any happier?

Shopping has become a virtual reality existence in which we simply try to copy the wealthiest ten percent of the population, whereas we'd be much better off realising that we're never going to have that kind of dosh and stop worrying about it.

As Duane Elgin, who is at the heart of the American downshifting movement says, it may well be worth our while actually making a "deliberate choice to live with less in the belief that more of life will be returned to us in the process" (*Voluntary Simplicity – Toward a Life that is Outwardly Simple, Inwardly Rich*, William Morrow,1993).

This is how we make our lives more expensive than they need to be. More really can mean less. If you have a pair of black shoes, you only need to have the polish and brushes to clean black shoes. Buy brown shoes and you need to buy the polish and brushes for them. With one colour of shoes, you only need to keep in one colour of spare laces. Almost every purchase you make sends you on a spiral of further purchasing. And buying things is an expensive business.

But it's not just buying things that is expensive, it's how we buy them. More and more of us are borrowing increasingly large sums of money to help us buy what we want. We're in debt up to our eye-balls and need a way out, which leads us to the next chapter.

Chapter 4:

Get Rid of the Debts

Annual income twenty pounds, annual expenditure nineteen nineteen and six, result happiness. Annual income twenty pounds, annual expenditure twenty pounds – nought and six, result misery.

Mr Micawber in *David Copperfield*
by Charles Dickens

Our ancestors of one hundred years ago would not recognise the way money works today. If we want something – a new car, a hi-fi system, a conservatory – we can buy it straightaway. We don't have to worry about the hassle of saving up for it. We finance much of what we buy using credit. Instead of having savings, we have bank loans, credit cards, store cards or overdrafts. It's so much easier flexing your plastic. But remember – buying things in this way is phenomenally expensive.

Owning lots of stuff is not a way of liberating your life – it quite often has the the opposite effect. There is no fulfilment to be had from owning it if it only leads to indebtedness. The more dependent you are on credit to finance your lifestyle, the less chance you will ever have of breaking out of the vicious circle of consumer spending and indebtedness.

According to David Boyle in his book *Funny Money – In Search of Alternative Cash* (HarperCollins, 1999), since 1990 we in Britain have spent more on servicing our debts than we have on food. By servicing our debts, Boyle means interest payments on loans, bank charges, mortgages and so on. In case you didn't grasp that, I'm going to repeat it. We spend more money paying for the privilege of being in debt than we do on what we eat.

The pressure's on again

The trouble is that we're not just spending our own money: we're spending other people's as well. In the same way that shops tempt us with their clever layouts, we are also tempted into debt by the signals that are given out by the society in which we live.

It starts with our young adults. There was a time when university tuition was free and most students received a grant to go into higher education. Now, a university educa-tion has to be funded by loans, rather than by grants (except for the very wealthy who can rely on their parents for income). No matter what your political views on this issue, there is one very important outcome. It gives eighteen year olds, who are only just beginning to struggle into adult-hood, the idea that it is all right to borrow now, because you can pay it all back at some time in the future. You can start adult life in debt, rather than in credit.

According to a Barclays Bank survey, by the end of an undergraduate university course, the average student will be £5,286 in debt. This means that recent graduates have to concentrate on paying off their debts before they can even start to think about setting foot on even the lowest rung of the property ladder.

On top of all that, the British are a nation of home-owners, rather than tenants. Most of us don't have the £100,000 or so in cash that you need to buy the average house in Britain, so we end up borrowing the money to pay for it in the shape of a mortgage. Banks and Building

Societies are quite happy to lend at least three times your annual salary to buy a house – often they will lend far more. First-time buyers often don't even have to produce any of their own money as a deposit and can borrow the full amount of the mortgage.

Credit comes easily. The banks encourage it with over-drafts, car loans and credit cards. The big stores produce their own charge cards, enabling you to buy goods you don't have the money to buy outright. Finance companies, often in co-operation with the big stores, love you to pay for goods over time – it brings them in more money. They all want you to go into debt to pay for your house, your car, your clothes, your furniture and even your groceries.

The strange thing about all this debt is that for a lot of us it is actually largely unnecessary. Again, just think of the frugality of our parents' generation. Household expenditure at constant prices has more than trebled in real terms between 1951 and 1998. Yet, despite the obvious increase in our personal wealth that this indicates, we do not seem to bother to do a great deal of saving. Thirty per cent of households have no savings at all. Perhaps this is under-standable. There are many people struggling by on low incomes and young people who are just starting out have other priorities. What is perhaps even more worrying is that, despite our enormous wealth, the average post-tax income in this country is nearly £15,000 per year – only 23% of households have more than £10,000 tucked away in savings.

The rise in the number of card transactions is perhaps indicative of the way we are going. A credit or debit card is such an easy way to pay for things. You don't part with actual, real, hard cash nor do you have to fiddle around filling out a cheque (and stub, if you're good). Between 1991 and 1998, we doubled the number of transactions that we put on our plastic cards and trebled the actual amount of money spent in this way.

By the end of 1998, our individual debts (with the honourable exception of mortgages) amounted to £101.4 billion – almost double the figure for 1987. To give you a rough idea, that means that, on average, every single one of us in the country, man, woman or child, is in debt to the tune of £1,700. What a waste of money.

We are lured into a new way of thinking. Logically, we should be asking the question, "Can I afford to buy that?" Instead, we ask ourselves, "Can I afford the monthly repayments on that?" Some of us don't even bother with that and launch ourselves into ridiculous levels of debt.

We are obviously a nation of spenders rather than savers.

How debt works

There are many different ways of getting into debt. The thing to bear in mind all the time is that debt is expensive. You not only pay interest on the amount you borrow, you also pay interest on the interest outstanding.

You will come across loans and credit cards being quoted with an APR. APR stands for Annual Percentage Rate. Imagine that your credit card charges 2% interest per month. You might expect that at the end of a year, you will have paid back the money at an annual rate of 24% – twelve months multiplied by 2% is 24%. What you haven't taken into account is the way in which compound interest affects debts.

Let's imagine that you borrowed ten thousand pounds at the beginning of January and did not pay anything back until the end of December. You are paying interest at 2% per month.

At the end of

January	you owe	£10,200
February	you owe	£10,404

March	you owe	£10,612.08
April	you owe	£10,824.32
May	you owe	£11,040.81
June	you owe	£11,261.62
July	you owe	£11,486.86
August	you owe	£11,716.59
September	you owe	£11,950.92
October	you owe	£12,189.94
November	you owe	£12,433.74
December	you owe	£12,682.41

Instead of the £2,400 you were expecting to pay in interest, you have had to pay £2,682.41 – quite a lot more. This is because of the simple fact that you have to pay interest on the interest. The APR in this case is nearer 27%.

What kind of a debtor are you?

There are all sorts of reasons why we tend to get into debt. Some of it is no doubt caused by poverty. However, for most of us, no matter how much we look to excuses for our financial situations, there are probably three main reasons why we are in debt.

The first is, quite simply, lack of discipline. Easy credit means that you are unlikely to starve to death if you run out of money. It doesn't occur to you that an ill-disciplined approach to your finances has a larger repercussion on your life. Ignoring basic budgeting is a recipe for indebtedness.

Secondly, many of us are buying in the forlorn hope that we are going to make ourselves happy by owning more.

Thirdly, call it what you like, but there is also a kind of greed or pride that makes us compare our situations with other people. The more possessions we have that make us seem prosperous, the more respect we hope to gain from other people. We are seeking some kind of status through our house, our car, our clothes or from where our children go to school. You can tell who we are from what we buy.

You have to realise that there are also three kinds of indebtedness – responsible indebtedness, problem indebtedness and compulsive indebtedness.

Responsible indebtedness is the kind of debt that one has to take in order to live in the modern world. If you want to purchase your own house, the chances are that you won't have enough money to be able to buy one outright. Buying a house that won't push you to the limits of your finances by using a mortgage is probably sensible indebtedness.

On the other hand, if you become over-ambitious in what you buy on credit, you might find yourself being over-stretched. You begin to have to pay a huge chunk of your monthly income on servicing your debt. You are now suffering from problem indebtedness. When your life becomes imbalanced like this, it is not the longest step in the world to becoming a compulsive debtor.

The compulsive debtor staggers from one debt crisis to the next. An opportunity to have another credit card has to be grabbed with both hands. One debt is used to pay for another in a merry-go-round of false optimism and financial mismanagement.

Our financial inertia means that we do not look for the best rates of interest for our savings, the least expensive options for our mortgages, the leanest financial product or the best credit card.

But horse-whipping yourself for getting into financial trouble isn't going to solve the problem and will only bring you added guilt. What you need to do is to sort out exactly where you stand and then do something about it.

You are now suffering from problem indebtedness.

How badly in debt are you?

If you're feeling a bit bruised from the last few paragraphs, then this is the point in the chapter where you might feel as though you want to skip and read on, or give up on the book altogether. However, if you're keen on the idea of leading a simpler life, you can't do so with the millstone of debt around your neck. Bluntly, you have to do two things: work out how much you're in debt and then devise a plan for dealing with it. There is no way around these two stages.

To get some idea of the extent of what you owe, grab a piece of paper and mark out the following grid:

Type of Debt	Monthly Repayment	Date of Final Payment	Total Amount Payable
Store Cards			
Credit Cards			
Bank Loans			
Hire Purchase Loans			
Debts to Friends or Family			
Money Lenders			
Mortgage			
Overdraft			
Interest Free Deals from Shops			
Catalogue Repayments			
Any Other Debt			
Total			

In the first column, write down the actual amount you have to pay each month for each of these types of payment. If you are paying weekly, multiply the amount by number of weeks in the year (52) and then divide by the number of months in a year (12) to get a figure. For instance if you are paying £20 per week, 20 × 52 = 1040. 1040 ÷ 12 = £86.67.

When you have done this, you then need to calculate how much is still outstanding on any of these loans. If you do not have the very latest figures from your bank or building society, you might have to work some of these out. To do this, simply multiply your monthly payments by the length of the loan. For instance, if your mortgage is £400 per month and you still have ten years and three months (in other words 123 months) to go, you need to multiply £400 by 123. The result is that you have roughly got another £49,200 to pay. I know that the mortgage rate is normally variable and that if interest rates fall, you could end up paying less than this, but don't forget that they can also rise, which would mean that you would have to pay even more.

How much do your debts cost you?

For most of us, the above exercise is a fairly bleak affair, but not the end of the world. You know how much you owe, but you don't know how much your debts are costing you.

For the next step you will need to get hold of your bank statements, latest mortgage statement, credit card statements, store card statements and so forth. If you can't get hold of them, because you've thrown them away or ignored them, then I suggest that you save the next ones as they come in for a time and do the same exercise, but using three months as the period.

Bank statements

Add together all the payments you have made to the bank for any agreed overdraft fee or account charges (normally you only have to pay these if the account is in the red).

Store cards and credit cards

Add together any annual fees and the total amount of interest you have paid.

Mortgage

On your mortgage statement there will be a list of how much you have paid to the lender. If you have a repayment mortgage, there will be a figure showing your outstanding balance at the beginning of the year and your outstanding balance at the end of the year. Subtract your current balance from the start of year balance to get the amount you have "paid off" your mortgage this year. Add together all your mortgage payments and then subtract this figure from the total.

e.g.   Balance at start of year =   £21,000

       Balance at end of year =   £20,000

       Total repaid =   £1,000

       12 monthly payments at £400 =   £4,800

       £4,800 – £1,000 = £3,800 =   total amount spent servicing the debt.

If you have an endowment mortgage, a pension mortgage or a PEP or ISA mortgage, all of your mortgage each month is going to service your debt as you are actually saving to pay off the original lump sum through the PEP or endowment or whatever. Simply record the amount you have paid in this way.

Bank loans and hire purchase

It is harder to work out the amount you are paying here, so we will use a technique that will essentially take the average amount of interest you will have paid. When you take out any loan, the first few payments are almost entirely swallowed up in interest. To make things easier for you, we are going to assume that you pay interest at the same rate across the loan. Find out how much the total repayment figure is and how much you paid for whatever it was you bought – car, hi-fi, whatever – and subtract it from the total amount payable. Then divide the remaining amount by the number of years of the contract.

e.g.   Total amount of loan =   £700

        Cost of item =   £400

        Interest amount =   £300

The loan is for three years, so £300 ÷ 3 = £100. In other words, you are paying an average of one hundred pounds each year for that particular loan.

And add it all together

When you have calculated all these figures, you will see how much money you are spending on servicing your borrowing. As a last calculation, work out what your income is each year after tax and then calculate what percentage of that income goes purely on servicing your debts.

If you really want to frighten yourself, work out how many hours a year you have to work just to pay for your debts. And remember debts are dead, useless money. You could actually be putting that money to good use.

If you have done all the things I have suggested, you are probably feeling in pretty low spirits. You are probably also looking for some explanations or excuses for your behaviour. "Well, a car like that only comes along once in a while." "I need a bit of a holiday now and then." "It was a bargain." "You've got to live somewhere." "It's nothing compared to how much John and Kate down the road owe."

All these may well be true, but at some point you have to realise that you are responsible for your own actions.

I know that there are certain debts that are hard to avoid – a mortgage is almost a necessity, but it is still your responsibility to make sure that you are going to get out of debt. If you ignore your debts, they will only get worse. You need to take some practical steps to get yourself back in the black.

A lot of people think that the best way to do this is to take out one larger loan from one lender and pay off all of the debts in one fell swoop. There is some logic to this. Credit cards and store cards charge very high rates of interest – a bank loan is probably a great deal cheaper.

If you honestly think that you are the kind of person who can do this and then be self-disciplined enough not to get into further debt, it might just work. However, debt counsellors normally advise against this course of action, because they fear you might simply start to accumulate more debts.

If you are so badly in debt that you cannot cope at all, the best thing to do is to make an appointment to see a counsellor at the Citizens' Advice Bureau. You should avoid bankruptcy if you possibly can. The CAB's counsellors are highly trained. Don't be afraid to visit them. They know how to negotiate with building societies, banks, finance houses and other creditors who might want to grab your house, car or valuables. Whatever happens, do not fall prey to either the loan sharks who demand extortionate rates of interest to clear off your debts or start borrowing from friends. It is a sure-fire way to lose them.

Back to basics

If you now feel that you owe more than you want and that you are paying out ridiculous sums of money servicing your debts, you probably want to do something about it. Unfortunately the cure for your problems is not a happy one. It involves more arithmetic (and you're probably fed up with that by now) and a great deal of self-discipline.

What you have to do is to write down absolutely every single penny that you spend.

I know it's time consuming, but it's the only way. There are computer programmes such as Quicken or Microsoft Money that will help you, but there's nothing quite like the physical sensation of writing it all down to help you to feel what you are doing.

Buy yourself a tiny little cashbook that will fit into your pocket. Every time you pay out any money for anything – even the silliest, tiniest amount – make a note of it in your book. This should include payments made by any method – cash, cheque, store card, credit card, direct debit, standing order, whatever. At the end of every evening, transfer what you have spent into either a larger ledger with appropriate headings, or use a computer programme such as those mentioned earlier or a spreadsheet.

The kinds of headings you might want to use are: Alcohol and tobacco; Cleaning; Clothing; Council Tax; Eating out; Electricity; Entertainment; Food; Gas; Gifts; Groceries; Hairdressing; Hobbies and sports; Holidays; Household; Medical; Mortgage/rent; Pets; Repairs; Servicing your debts (except mortgage); Takeaways; Tax; Telephone; Transport; Water rates.

Don't be afraid to come up with your own headings. Then add up what you spend in any given month. After a while, you will soon see a pattern to your spending.

Here's the plan

You now know what you are spending on various items. Look through your list and see if there are any items that you could honestly do without.

For instance, if you smoke twenty cigarettes a day, you will find that you are spending about £140 per month on cigarettes. There is an obvious answer – stop smoking. However, as an ex-smoker myself (I know, they're the worst kind), I know just how difficult it is to give up. If you do smoke, now is the best time to give up. If you can't do it on your own, join a group or a class at your local health centre. Get your GP to help.

It's not just a question of smoking. There will be a host of silly indulgences that are keeping you from managing your money properly and merely serving to keep you in debt. Decide where you can make those savings.

Your house

If you are very good and your only debt is your mortgage, you might think about re-paying your mortgage at an earlier stage. Paying off a mortgage is a great step towards simplifying your life. If you earn £2,000 per month net and £500 of your hard-earned money goes on paying for the mortgage, you are working nearly one week every month just to pay for the roof over your head. Why on earth would you want to increase your repayments to £1,000 per month when that would mean having to work for almost two weeks in every month just to pay for it? The answer is simple – you will pay off your mortgage much more quickly.

There was a time when there were certain tax advantages to having a mortgage. You got tax relief on a proportion of the interest you paid. However, that has all changed and the government no longer subsidises your house purchase. Nowadays, it makes sense to repay a mortgage in the shortest possible time available to you. If you have a straightforward "repayment" mortgage, this is quite easily done. It can be slightly more complex with a mortgage that is linked to an investment device, such as an endowment plan.

To keep things relatively simple, we will stick with a repayment mortgage. If your Building Society is lending money at a rate of 7.35%, the monthly cost of this loan will vary enormously, depending on the length of your mortgage.

Mortgage Term	Monthly Payment per £1,000	Total Payable per £1,000
10 years	£12.06	£1,447.20
15 years	£9.36	£1,684.80
20 years	£8.09	£1,941.60
25 years	£7.38	£2,214.00

Put another way, if you pay off a mortgage in ten years rather than in twenty-five, you will save £766.80 for every £1,000 of your mortgage. Let's suppose that you are just about to take out a mortgage for £50,000. What difference would it make to you if you paid it off over a shorter period than is usual?

Mortgage Term	Monthly Payment	Total Payable
10 years	£603.00	£72,360.00
15 years	£468.00	£84,240.00
20 years	£404.50	£97,080.00
25 years	£369.00	£110,700.00

You don't need to be an eagle-eyed scout to spot that there is a whacking great difference between what you have to repay if you have a mortgage over ten years compared to one over twenty-five years. You would have to pay an additional £38,340. However, it's important to be realistic. You might well not be able to afford to pay £603 per month to take advantage of the cheapest way of repaying your mortgage. However, you might be able to manage the £404.50. In which case, by repaying your mortgage five years earlier than you had planned, you would still save £13,620 – which is not to be sniffed at.

Perhaps most importantly of all, the sooner you have paid off your mortgage, the sooner you have the luxury of living in what is essentially rent-free accommodation.

Repay as quickly as you can

Smaller loans work in a similar fashion to mortgages. If you borrow £5,000, then the speed with which you repay the loan will determine how much or how little that loan will cost you. For instance, if you borrow that £5,000 over seven years at an APR of 12.9%, you will be paying over £2,000 more in interest than you would do if you paid it back within a year.

Period of Loan	7 years	3 years	1 year
Monthly Repayment	£88.82	£166.62	£444.99
Total Repayable	£7,461.30	£5,998.28	£5,339.79
Cost of Loan	£2,461.30	£998.28	£339.79

If you insure the loan, so that it will be repaid should you fall ill or become redundant, for instance, the costs are even greater.

Problems arise when you view a smallish sum, such as

£88.82 per month, as being easily within your financial reach. It may be; but do you really want to be paying back almost half as much again for the loan? This applies to any kind of loan you take out. Your mortgage is probably the largest loan you will ever have and it will take a long time to repay.

Store cards and credit cards

If you have difficulty curbing your spending on these, the only thing to do is to cut them up and send them back to the companies who issued you with them. If you have a lot of debt on your card, you could transfer it to another card which charges a lower rate of interest. Beware, however, of the danger I mentioned earlier of simply finding a new way to increase your debts. A cheaper-rate credit card should replace your existing one, not work alongside it.

Used sensibly, a credit card is a useful way of shopping. It normally provides you with anything up to fifty days or so of interest-free credit.

Cash

Pay cash for as many things as you can. There are two good reasons for this. First, cash feels like real money and so there is the psychological effect of parting with real money. Secondly, if you pay cash for things, you may often be able to get a discount. By this, I don't mean that you can avoid paying VAT to the plumber. If you buy something in a shop using a credit card, the shop will have to pay a percentage of the amount you have spent to the credit card company. If you point this out whilst paying, some shops will often give you a small discount.

Avoid further debt to pay off existing debts

Most debt advisors reckon that taking out a large single loan to pay off other outstanding debts is a bad move. I suspect that they find that what happens is that people just end up with all the existing debts and the added disadvantage of a brand new one.

If your credit rating is particularly poor, you might also find yourself being tempted to borrow from the kind of moneylenders who tour housing estates on a weekly basis. According to the Rowntree Foundation, the APR on loans from moneylenders can be anything from 100% to 500%. Nor do moneylenders knock around in a wolf's disguise anymore – most collectors are women and they operate on the basis of befriending their customers; ironically the kind of "relationship banking" that the High Street banks used to work on, until they stopped being in the High Street.

Don't forget that any debts that you have can be negotiated.

Look to the future

A life without debt is, I can promise you, far nicer than one in which you are weighed down by constant repayments. Debt is bad for you. At Ohio State University, academics have established that there is a link between high levels of debt and extreme stress, which in its turn leads to heart attacks, irrational patterns of thinking, an inability to control emotions and loss of concentration.

Above all, how on earth are you ever going to downshift if you're surrounded by red letters, credit card slips and angry letters from a faceless bank manager?

Chapter 5:

Get Rid of the Clutter

Man must choose whether to be rich in things or in the freedom to use them.

Ivan Illich

Three and a half years after we moved into our current house, we decided to convert the cellar into an office. It seemed an excellent idea. Not only would we be making the best use of the space we had available, but we would also be freeing our lives of some clutter. If you've ever had a house with a cellar, you'll probably have a good idea of what ours was like. The carcasses of old kitchen units, plastic plant pots, an implement that defies any explanation as to its use, but which you certainly wouldn't want to fall into the hands of a psychopath; all of it strung together with cobwebs. In amongst all the dusty boxes and crumpled carrier bags, I came across two boxes that bore the name of the removals company. Inside were empty jam jars. We didn't even know they were there.

Now, empty jam jars are not the worst thing that you can save – after all, making your own jam is one of life's great pleasures. But to have carted two box loads nearly four hundred miles, not used them for forty-odd months, and to have paid for the privilege of so doing was ridiculous.

I suspect that fewer of us nowadays do as thorough a spring-clean as previous generations did, which means that our houses become home to a ton of broken odds and ends – and they are supposed to be homes for us. We are also earning a great deal more than previous generations and have access to objects and luxuries undreamt of in a previous age.

Look around your home. Be honest with yourself. How much of the stuff in your house do you ever use? Having too many things only means that you end up with tons of clutter everywhere, making the place far harder to clean. I'm not advocating that you should live in a house with no possessions. What I am suggesting is that all your possessions count for something – that they serve some purpose.

There are individuals in some of the big cities who will advise on how to streamline your life to get rid of the clutter. They will charge you a huge fee for it. Let me help you on your path to a simpler, less expensive life, by explaining a straightforward method of streamlining your home. You can put the money you have saved by not hiring an expert to do this for you into a savings account.

Essentially, you should look on the clutter in your house as being just that – clutter. To paraphrase Don Aslett, from his book *Clutter's Last Stand*, the problem with clutter is that:

- It makes every job take longer. You have to sift through oodles of stuff simply to find what you want.
- It means that ordinary household tasks take longer. The more things you own, the more things you have to clean round or under or over.
- If you imagine your house as a storage warehouse, just think how much you are spending on the heating and lighting needed in all those extra rooms to contain the clutter.
- And owning things is hazardous. It invites burglars (and higher insurance premiums), provides fuel for house fires and is the perfect way in which to cause a domestic accident.

Get busy

I suggest that you allow yourself a fortnight for each room of the house. Some rooms will take longer; some less. If you have the kind of garage which has never been uncluttered enough to fit the car in anyway, you may find that you have to spend more time there.

Go through each room with a fine toothed comb, identifying what possessions you have.

First of all, ask yourself if you really need an item. There are different levels of need. Not everything you need is necessarily a highly practical item. You don't want to get rid of the picture above the fireplace just because you can't use it for straining spaghetti or fixing the brakes on the car. If you like having nice pictures on your walls, fair enough. You may have a hat that you only ever wear to weddings. If you think you need that hat, it's worth keeping, because even though you don't use it for months or possibly years on end, it still has a practical purpose. Alternatively, you could always decide you don't need it often enough and go bareheaded.

Be strict with yourself. Most of us build up collections of videos and CDs and, although we may like a lot of what we buy, there are often several CDs we wouldn't play from one year to the next and videos that we have already watched and are never likely to do so again. The same is true with loads of our possessions all over the house, garage and garden.

If you no longer need or use something, then there are basically three courses of action open to you. You can sell the item, you can give it away or you can throw it out.

Clothing

I suspect that there is more unused stuff in the bedroom than in any other room in the house. Most of the stuff we have in our bedrooms is clothes and I wonder how many we really still wear.

Avoid extremes of fashion.

If you buy the best quality clothes you can afford, and as few as you can practically get away with, then your clothes should last you for years. Avoid extremes of fashion and buy classic cuts whenever possible.

When buying clothes, ask yourself exactly how much wear you are going to get out of a particular item. If you are only going to wear it once in a blue moon, then don't buy it.

Always buy in the sales if possible, but don't buy something just because it's reduced in price. Avoid buying anything that needs dry-cleaning. It's an expensive business.

Go through your wardrobe and divide the contents into the following piles:

- Clothes that are incredibly tatty.
- Clothes that are OK, but you normally wouldn't wear.
- Clothes that are OK, but no longer fit you.
- Clothes that need repairing.
- Clothes you still wear.

Clothes that are incredibly tatty

If they are really very tatty indeed, you can use them as rags in the kitchen or garage. If you can't even see them being any use for this, either chuck them out, or find out if there is anywhere locally that recycles fabrics. In the larger towns, you may still get the odd rag-and-bone man. I'm not sure how much you'd get for them, but at least they'll be put to some use.

Clothes that are OK, but you would no longer wear

It may be that the orange tank top and deep purple shirt with big rounded collars are still in great condition, but for some reason, you simply wouldn't like to be seen wearing them in public. Simply wear them for doing work such as painting, gardening or DIY work. If you can't even bring yourself to do that, give them to charity or someone you know who goes to a lot of seventies discos or earns their living as a Gilbert O'Sullivan impersonator.

Clothes that are OK, but no longer fit you

If, like me, you can't rely on your waistline to stay where it was, then you've got two choices. Either you can hang on to these in the hope that when you do lose weight they'll fit you again, or you can bite the bullet, accept the fact you're never going to do it and get rid of them.

If they are very smart clothes, especially clothes with well-known labels, you might find that there is a shop or a dress agency locally that will try to sell them on your behalf. You could also try car-booting better clothing. If you can't shift them for money, then either give them to friends who welcome that sort of thing – students in the family are usually always on the scrounge for something – or give them all to charity. Many re-cycling sites now have a container where you can place unwanted clothes.

Clothes that need repairing

Well, I think you know what I'm going to tell you. Yes, that's right: if they're worth repairing do it, if not throw them out. Sewing on buttons is child's play, although you might find repairing tears and darning a little tougher. If it's beyond you, see if you can find a friend who will do it for you in return for some little skill of yours.

Clothes you still wear

If you genuinely still wear it, put it back in the wardrobe. If you're not sure if you wear it or not, take a piece of paper and write the date on it and then pin it to the item in question. The next time you do this trick with your wardrobe, see if you've worn the particular item in the last six months. If you haven't then you obviously don't want it.

The garage and the garden shed (and possibly the cellar again)

It's a strange fact, but leave a couple of garden tools lying around and, just like wire coat-hangers, they will breed. In no time at all you will find that they have taken over all the available space. Sheds and garages have an unnatural propensity to fill up with broken shelf brackets, rusty screws, windscreen wipers with perished rubbers that came off a car you sold in 1969, a cassette player with a broken sprocket and several gunged-up paintbrushes in a variety of exciting 1970s oranges and beiges.

Go on, get in there. Be ruthless. If you want to sort your various little bits and pieces, such as screws, nails, rawl plugs or whatever, you can buy yourself one of those neat sets of plastic drawers. A cheaper alternative is to keep your used coffee jars (although not in the cellar for three and a half years) and divide all your bits and pieces into them. If you then screw the lids to the underside of a shelf in your shed or garage or whatever, you have not only saved the top of the shelf for larger items, but you've made your life more organised and re-used something that might otherwise simply go into a landfill site.

If you're the kind of person who has cluttered every spare inch of garden and driveway with cars that no longer work in the forlorn belief that one day you might just put them back on the road, or that those Ford Anglia spares just might come in handy on a Citroën, then shame on you. All you are doing is making your neighbourhood look like a rubbish tip. Why should your neighbours suffer from your appalling scruffiness? Get yourself organised and get them all carted off to the scrap yard or, if you've got something that might genuinely be of interest to a collector, get it sold.

If you own two or more cars, you should make the tough decision as to whether or not you really need them. Selling cars can be a difficult business. You will find magazines at your local newsagent that give a guide to prices. Selling can be done through advertising on notice-boards, local papers, specialist "for sale" newspapers, or by sticking a piece of paper on the rear passenger windows. If it is a particularly sought-after make of car, there may be a hobbyist publication with small ad pages. A clean, tidy and smart car is much more likely to sell than one that is grimy or covered in cow-muck. Yes, I know that's stating the obvious, but you'd be surprised how many people don't smarten up their jalopy before putting it up for sale.

The kitchen, larder and utility room

If you're a bit of a gadget freak you may find that you have collected together more kitchen devices than you could possibly ever imagine using. I have a pet theory that people own kitchen gadgets in inverse proportion to their ability as cooks. Visit any kitchen that boasts electric can-openers, waffle-makers, sushi coolers or whatever and you can bet that you're in the house of someone who thinks a King Edward is a cigar.

Be honest with yourself. Excess gadgetry just means that you need several extra acres of work surface and a larger kitchen. Evaluate each device you've got and, if you think you don't get enough use out of it, sell it to someone who feels the need to clutter up their own work surfaces.

Similarly, explore the darkest recesses of your larder and get rid of anything that is well beyond its sell-by date. If you make a list of all the food you have in your larder and freezer and find that you have enough to feed a small army, then use it all up now, before any of it goes off. Strangely enough, with all the modern methods we have for conserving and preserving our food – chilling and freezing especially – we do seem to let enormous quantities of the stuff go to waste.

Have a week or a month when you eat out your reserve stocks and see if you save yourself any money. Ask yourself if you really do need four months' worth of emergency rations if you only get bad snows once a year.

The bathroom

Do you really still need that threadbare towel at the bottom of the airing cupboard that you never use? Old towels are great as floor cloths, dog towels, emergency mops and so on. Use them up.

If you find that the bathroom cabinet is full of old half-finished medicines, take them to your pharmacist for safe disposal. Flushing tablets for illnesses long forgotten down the loo can be dangerous. There might even be a local collection point for old drugs where charities use them in developing countries.

Old spectacles are another bit of unnecessary hoarding. Always keep your last pair of spectacles as a spare pair in case you break your current ones. Beyond that, it's not worth hanging onto other old pairs unless you do amateur dramatics. It's fairly pointless hanging onto the things, especially if your prescription has changed a lot. Some countries in the developing world don't have access to optical care on the same level as we do, so old specs are often very welcome. Find out if your local Oxfam shop, doctor or optician collects them – they often do. If not, they probably know of other organisations that would be able to make use of them.

The study

A study, whether it is a room on its own or a corner of a spare bedroom, has the amazing property of acting like a paper magnet. No sooner do you turn your back on the place, than it fills up again with old electricity bills, offers of a time share in Biarritz, photographs you last saw in the mid-nineteen sixties (showing you in the same clothes that are still in your wardrobe) and money-off vouchers that expired sometime in the early part of the last decade.

You have to be really strict with yourself with a study, even if it simply consists of a table in the bedroom or a corner of your kitchen.

It seems very easy to collect pens, biros, felt tips and pencils. You pick them up off counters accidentally or get sent dozens through the post by charities or pen companies wanting your business. If you're anything like me, you probably end up with thousands of them. Gather all of them up from where they have been scattered around the house and have a sort out. Try them all out on a scrap of paper. Throw out the useless ones, give any that you don't need to the local school or, if they are fountain pens you never use, sell them at a car boot sale. Make sure that any pens you do keep, you will actually use and put them in convenient places, such as by the telephone.

As for that mountain of books, if you are a book-lover you will probably find it hard to part with any of them. If you are like that, then you too will end up with shelves of books, some of which you will never (if you are to be honest) read and some of which you will never re-read. Free up enough space on one set of shelves to put all the books you have yet to read. Try the first few pages of each and, if you think you'll read them, hang on to them. If you find you can't get into them, add them to the pile of books you will never read again; then they are ready for sale or disposal. Magazines (if not collectors' items) can go to your doctor's or dentist's surgery. They always seem to want magazines – especially really old ones.

I suspect that everyone has a bit of a pile of bills, odd bits of post, circulars and the general hotchpotch of what slips onto our doormats every day of the week. If you develop the good time management habit of taking action every time you get a piece of paper, it will save you a lot of clutter and a lot of heartache. Essentially, there are three things you can do with a piece of paper: deal with it, file it away somewhere or get rid of it. If you get rid of it, see if it can be recycled. Flyers, which are often blank on one side, are fine for note-pads that you can keep by the phone. Large envelopes can be used for filing things that you need to hang on to. Everything else you should act on as soon as you possibly can. A tax return unfilled feels like a Damoclesian sword over your head. Fill it out and send it in and you've not only dealt with the form, but can now file away all those bits of financial information that you'd been stock-piling in order to complete the form.

The sitting-room and dining-room

If you have electrical items you no longer want, you can try to sell them. Even old hi-fi systems are worth a few pounds – people with record collections on vinyl are always on the look out for something to play them on. Car-booting these items is not always very successful as people can't test out what they're buying, so you might find it easier to get rid of cheaper things through the "under £50" or equivalent section of your local paper, where the adverts are free. Unwanted furniture can also be sold this way. If, for whatever reason, you are thinking of using old furniture in a house you are going to rent out, then you need to check that they comply with the latest regulations – especially when it comes to settees, beds and easy chairs.

Stop reading and get sorting

I expect that as soon as you're faced with the idea of de-junking your house, you start falling back on a number of excuses. You just might get round to ... sentimental value ... might come in handy ... never know when you might need ... it was my mother's ... might be worth something someday ... These are all very well, but are nothing more than excuses. Clutter can damage your health, your wealth and wreak havoc with your time management. However, if you wanted to up the stakes and get a little more spiritual about these matters, you could quote almost every religion that has ever been. Religions tend to promote the idea of living a simpler life with fewer material possessions. If you like, the art of shedding material possessions is a means of simplifying your life: simplifying it from material worries and adding into it a spiritual dimension.

On the other hand, you might just fancy the idea of a good clear-out. There's money in all that unwanted stuff and, besides, you've still got all those debts to pay off from the previous chapter.

Selling

If you're a dab hand at selling things, then you might do very nicely indeed if you are embarking on a de-cluttering spree. If you are not used to selling, then don't imagine that you have to be a wide-boy or a bit of a shyster to sell off your unwanted stuff.

You are not simply selling things in order to raise money. You are also selling unwanted possessions because it creates space and it will also help you towards feeling less dependent on material goods for your happiness. So, you may not have to worry too much that you are getting the best price for a particular item.

Recently, for example, I sold a portable computer that had cost me £200 for only £10. You could look on this as a loss of £190 and, to an extent, you would be right. I had used it a fair amount, but it was old technology and had been superseded by a newer computer. By the time I came to sell it, all it was doing was taking up space in my study. Had I continued to leave it there, I would have got no money for it whatsoever. I'd prefer to think that I got £10 for something I no longer used and cleared some shelf-space into the bargain.

I guess that sometimes we think that because we paid a lot for something, we shouldn't sell it for next to nothing, so we end up hanging onto it, perhaps anticipating that we are going to get our money's worth from the object purely by owning it. This is the same type of logic that dictates that when you go to the cinema and the film is excruciatingly boring, you have to stay to the end because you've paid for your ticket.

The idea of getting your money's worth out of something is a good one. But it is an idea that you should apply _before_ you buy something and not afterwards.

Sometimes it hurts to get rid of stuff, not because it is of any use to you, but because it just shows you that you should have been more clever when you went shopping and not bought the thing in the first place.

On the other hand, if you decide that you are going to sell a diamond ring and you discover that it is worth £500, then you're not going to sell it for £5 just so as to have a bit more space. It may well be that you have to settle for £450, but you are still getting something approaching what you would reasonably expect.

When you sell your unwanted items, it is best to consider the most appropriate way in which to sell them. That £500 diamond ring isn't going to sell itself at a car-boot sale. For a start everyone will assume it's stolen and people don't go to car-boot sales to part with £500; they are looking for less pricey bargains.

Private advertisements in local papers, specialist small ads papers such as _Loot_ or its local equivalent are probably the best way of selling items such as an old guitar, a dish-washer, ageing stereo systems, forgotten golf clubs or unwanted furniture. Often your local shop or supermarket will have a notice board where you can advertise either free of charge or for a few pence.

Specialist items, such as jewellery, watches or the 7mm replica of the Tay Rail Bridge Disaster that has been gathering dust in the loft, are probably best sold through either specialist magazines or shops. Sometimes you may find that there is a thriving second-hand trade in what you want to get rid of. Some old toys, for instance, are now worth a packet, but often only if you kept the original packaging and never played with the toy itself – the tiniest paint chip can halve its value. Shops and traders dealing in these kinds of things are never going to offer you the full market rate. Why should they? After all, they have overheads to meet and they are taking the risk that they might not be able to sell it on to someone else.

For smaller items, such as books, old crockery, pots and pans, unwanted games and toys, in fact almost anything portable and inexpensive, your best way of making some money is the car-boot or tabletop sale. Make sure that everything you take is clean, including yourselves. Take a cloth to cover your table and try to make everything you are selling as neat as possible. Think like a trader. There are people who like to rummage so have a box of bits for them to fiddle around in. Other people like to see what they are getting. Display as much as you can so as to lure in as many potential buyers as possible. It is also a good idea to dress appropriately. Dress too scruffily and people will think you live in a hovel, assume all you have to sell is going to be filthy and not come near you. Dress as though it's Ascot week and everyone will assume that you can afford to give the stuff away. Clean jeans and a sweatshirt are ideal. Don't forget to make up a float of change: the first person to buy something from you inevitably only has a twenty-pound note.

Before you do a car-boot sale, visit a few as a customer (but try not to buy – you're supposed to be avoiding parting with money). Get to know the kinds of prices that are being charged for various things. Then, when it comes to your sale, you can price your own stuff sensibly. There's no point pricing things too highly – this is a car-boot sale, not a Knightsbridge department store – nor, for that matter, giving them away too cheaply.

Put price labels on all your bits and pieces and, during the course of the sale, move things around your stall a few times. Many people go round and round the stalls and it means that things that get overlooked on one circuit might get picked up on the next. Above all, be prepared to accept a reasonable offer.

If you live somewhere busy and can withstand the idea of having strangers all over your property, you might like the idea of a garage sale. If you can do such a thing, it's a great way of getting rid of all sorts of different stuff. It means that you don't have to cart around heavier items like garden equipment or furniture. People can also try out electrical goods, something they can't always do at a car-boot sale.

Raising money from unwanted items is a positive step forward. It does several things at the same time: it frees your house of stuff you don't want; it shows you how much you have spent in the past on unnecessary items and it brings in a little extra income.

It's worth being quite disciplined in this. If you think it's not a bad idea to sell anything that you no longer want, then try to keep a list of the items you need to sell. Anything that might go into a car-boot sale you can put into boxes in the loft so that they do not get in the way of your day-to-day living. It is probably worth doing a car-boot or tabletop sale every couple of months (you won't sell everything at one go) and if you have things that haven't sold after two or three sales, then you can give them to charity.

So, if you do all this, you should have a house that is tidier, with far less clutter; if you're really lucky, you'll have more money stashed away to make that big step into down-shifting and a few local charities will benefit. Everyone's a winner.

Chapter 6:

Get Rid of the Boss

Englishmen never will be slaves: they are free to do whatever the government and public opinion allow them to do.

George Bernard Shaw

I am constantly amazed by the number of people who continue to work at jobs they hate. They will find every excuse in the book to avoid doing anything about it. If they do change jobs, it is often to do the same thing, perhaps at a slightly promoted position. After the honeymoon period, they find that they hate what they are doing just as much as before – sometimes even more because they'd assumed that a promotion would bring with it an improvement in their lives and it didn't. Only this time, their bigger salary means that they have a bigger mortgage and a smarter car. They are now even more locked in to the rat race.

Huge numbers of us work ridiculously hard in order to create a future for ourselves at some distance down the line, when we can take things easy, put our feet up and enjoy the fruits of our labours.

The trouble is that there may not be as much fruit as we'd hoped. We've already seen in Chapter 2 how much of our time goes into sustaining ourselves in our work. It's very easy to eat the fruits as you go along, only to find that you don't have as much left as you'd have liked and that you're too old to enjoy what you've got left anyway.

So, it's all very well sitting in meetings, staring into space wondering what it would be like to lead a different life, but if you are determined to do something about it, you need to take action. Staring out of the window just doesn't help.

However, do not rush into anything too foolish just yet. Downshifting may not be for you and you don't want to throw away a career just because you've had a bad day at the office.

Before contemplating what you want to do, you need to decide what it is you don't like about what you do now. It may be that all you need is a change of employer, or a change of role within the same company. Don't just chuck in your job on a whim; think about it first.

Although many of us are working crazy hours, there are some employers who are beginning to listen to their employees. They are aware that an employee who has his or her life in balance is much more likely to be an effective and efficient worker. Some of them are also already getting the message that longer hours do not necessarily bring with them greater productivity. There is even a government initiative called "Work-life Balance" which has recognised the problem and is inviting employers to do something about it.

You could start by simply keeping to "normal" office hours. If you are lucky, your contract might state the number of hours you are expected to work. Try sticking to it for a week and see how you get on. One of the principles devised by C. Northcote Parkinson in his wonderful book *Parkinson's Law or The Pursuit of Progress* is that "Work expands so as to fill the time available for its completion". He gives the example of the elderly lady of leisure who, with nothing else to do all day than write a postcard, finds that the writing of the postcard does in fact take all day. You too might find that you have been wasting time and are perfectly capable of doing the job within your contracted hours.

You might also like to consider changing your job to a part-time job or doing a job-share. This might seem an unusual step for a man to take, but women have been doing it automatically for years. I know that sometimes part-timers don't get the recognition they deserve, but if all you are worried about is how you are perceived by other people, then you probably shouldn't even be contemplating down-shifting. After all, how are other people going to react when you start driving round in an old car and wearing your clothes until they fall apart?

If you have the kind of job that lends itself to working from home, you might like to approach your manager and see if it would be possible to do so. There are certain dangers in working from home, as we shall see later, but with modern conveniences such as fax, phone, computers, e-mail and the like, many jobs can easily be done at home. Some managers may worry that if you are at home you are not going to be working. However, if you have a good track record at your place of work, it might be possible to use a little persuasion, or you might be able to come to some kind of compromise. You might also worry that you are going to lose contact with your colleagues and co-workers, which is a more difficult argument to overcome. Perhaps you can achieve some kind of compromise that enables you to work at home for part of the week? Alternatively, you could start off by working at home for one day a week and then gradually increase the time spent there. If your employer is flexible enough to allow you to do this, then you might have to show some kind of flexibility in return, such as going into the office from time to time and covering for other staff when they are absent.

Telecommuting requires discipline and, like a small home-based business, appropriate space, machinery, materials, equipment and reference materials. Above all, telecommuting is not a simple way to replace genuine childcare or even the downshifter's version of childcare, which always used to be called parenting.

In fact, managers should fear little from allowing people to work from home. Studies show that people work much more effectively there. There are normally fewer interruptions (unless you have very small children) and people who do work at home often boast about how much more productive they have become.

Ah, but . . .

On the other hand, you might not be able to re-organise your existing job or find a new job, or perhaps you are just so sick of what you are doing that you need a complete break. Perhaps the time has come for you to examine your job in depth.

Get yourself a sheet of paper, rule a line down the middle, and down one side of the page write down everything you dislike about your job and on the other side everything you like. The kinds of things you might either like or dislike could include the routine, the boss, commuting, meetings, your colleagues, the social life, the actual office environment, your clients, aspects of your actual work.

Keep the list in a safe and private place and add to it when anything else occurs to you. When you look at this list, you may well think that perhaps your job isn't so bad after all or that you simply need a change of company. After all, we all go through bad patches.

However, if your "likes" column contains little items such as "the coffee, my desk, the free calendar I get every year" and the "dislikes" column contains everything of importance, then maybe it is time for a complete break.

If you would feel more secure as an employee, then there is nothing wrong in looking round for another job. It might be absolutely great to go from a demanding job to something rather more straightforward. In the film *American Beauty*, Kevin Spacey ends up flipping hamburgers rather than working for a company that manages its staff on the basis of the fear of redundancy.

What about an off-the peg business?

You might like to think about buying a franchise or an existing business. I know several people who have bought existing businesses and a handful who have bought franchises. I'm not sure whether any of them would say that they now have an easier life; in fact, most would say that they are busier and having to work even longer hours. But the ones who have made a success of it are much happier than they ever were before. If you are thinking about buying an existing business, you may need a considerable amount of capital, which might again defeat the whole idea that you had in the first place – that of taking life more easily.

You could also consider a franchise. The British Franchise Association defines a franchise as "the granting of a licence by one person (the franchiser) to another (the franchisee) to trade under the trade mark/trade name of the franchiser and to make use of an entire package, comprising all the elements necessary to establish a previously untrained person in the business and to run it with continual assistance on a predetermined basis". The advantage here is that you can retrain to do something new and, at the same time, you have a chance of investigating a franchise to see if you think you could do it and if you think it is a viable proposition. A successful franchise has a proven formula and will probably increase your chances of success. There are over 30,000 of them in this country now, employing over 300,000 people. According to the BFA, approximately 30% of all retail sales are in franchised businesses. It's a growing sector of the economy.

Franchises are increasingly popular and they range from chains of hamburger restaurants to photocopying shops, from cleaning services to carpeting retailers, air conditioning to windscreen replacement, couriers to car breakdown services.

Start your own business

If you now think that the time has come to go it alone, then you need to start thinking about your own skills.

If there is something you have always longed to do, now is the time to do it. Perhaps you've always loved model trains, made silver jewellery in your spare time, built dolls' houses or love gardening. Similarly, many people leave the company they work for, having built up a whole load of contacts over the years, and then sell their skills to their old company and use their network of contacts elsewhere to build up their own portfolio of clients.

If you are one of those lucky people, then you've probably got a fair idea of what you want to do. The rest of us are less fortunate. We don't have a sense of vocation, the capital to buy a business or a list of potentially lucrative contacts that we can put to good use. We may also, quite frankly, be so fed up with the area or specialism that we have developed that we want a clean break from it all.

We spend most of our lives underestimating our own abilities. We also get channelled into thinking that we can only do one sort of job. Now is the time for you to start thinking what you could do for yourself, not what you could do for other people. Do not hide your light under a bushel. Remind yourself – you are your greatest asset.

I always find it useful to make lists. If you can't stand doing things this way, then I'm sure that you will be creative enough to come up with your own way of generating ideas. If you can live with lists, then do the following. Be warned –

you're going to need plenty of paper for this. If you feel like being good, you should use the blank side of some scrap paper.

Get hold of six good-sized sheets of paper and at the top of each sheet write one of the following:

- My strengths.
- My experiences.
- My hobbies and interests.
- My skills.
- I am excited by.
- I have achieved.

Lay all the sheets of paper on a table and as things occur to you, write them on to the relevant sheet. If you need prompting for ideas, rope in your husband, wife or partner. Get the kids to help. Dig out your CV. Flick through photograph albums. Ring up old friends. Get out that box from the loft with your old school reports in.

Try to write things down as quickly as possible. Don't worry if things are duplicated, if a hobby ends up on the strengths list or your experience and achievement lists overlap. Avoid numbering any of the items on your list as that might make the first things that you think of seem more important than things that occur to you later. It doesn't matter either if your writing is all over the page. In fact, the more jumbled up everything is the better. The idea is to get as many positive things about yourself and what you have done down onto a piece of paper. And it doesn't matter how trivial these things are - you will see why later.

Again, keep these pieces of paper handy; you can add to them at any stage. Eventually, you should have dozens of words, ideas and little phrases down on your sheets. Now, you could start to be scientific about this next stage and rank everything according to what you enjoyed best or what your greatest achievement has been.

However, if you really want to play around for ideas for what you could do for work in the future, why not try this trick. Get a load of small index cards, or cut some paper into that kind of size, and write down each of the items from your master list onto the cards, using one card per idea. If you have been very thorough, you will end up with an enormous pile. Shuffle them as though they were playing cards and then break the pack up into two, three or even four piles. Turn over one card from each pile and see what you get. The reason that you are doing this is because in that way you are putting together two or more ideas that you would not normally associate with one another. With luck, you will end up with some brand new ideas that are formed by putting together two or more totally unrelated ideas.

For instance, say you enjoy horse-riding and you also like going on holiday. You turn over one card that says "Junior Gymkhana Champion" and another that says "French Holiday". From this could come a host of ideas for what you might do. And don't dismiss the silliest of ideas, sometimes they create new ideas of their own. From these two words, you might come up with the following suggestions for a new career:

- Organising riding holidays in France.
- Importing French horses.
- Exporting horses to France.
- Importing/exporting riding equipment.
- Exercising horses for people who are away on holiday.
- Opening a riding stables.
- Opening a riding shop.
- Organising riding holidays in England for French horse lovers.

I'm sure you could add more ideas to the list.

Repeat this exercise. Shuffle the cards, try new combinations. Try it with three piles, then with four. Write down all the ideas that come to you, no matter how stupid they may seem. It can be a good idea doing this exercise with other people. The technique of generating ideas is called "brainstorming". It can be a very powerful tool indeed. But remember, it works best if you do not comment on people's ideas as you list them. Include ridiculous and preposterous ideas at this stage.

Then, after you can face doing this no more, go through your list of ideas (which should be pretty impressive) and pick out the ones that have some mileage.

Let's imagine we're working from the list above we made from being a junior gymkhana champion and your holiday in France. If you don't speak particularly good French, organising things for English people in France or French people in England could be a bit tricky. Importing and exporting might be a problem too. On the other hand, you might know someone with brilliant French with whom you could team up.

If you don't have any capital, then opening a riding shop or stable is out of the question; unless, of course, you are prepared to go into debt. And wait a minute, if you're prepared to go into debt, are you really going to be downshifting or are you merely going to be trading one set of problems for another? Perhaps you don't really want to downshift at all, but would be happier going into business in a "serious" way?

You might settle for the idea of providing a horse exercising service for people who are away on holiday. It may not be what you end up doing, but at least it's a possibility.

If you do this for all the combinations of ideas that you come up with, you should eventually have a list of ideas that are both feasible and that you think you would be interested in doing. And that is vitally important. If you are going to downshift and genuinely cope with less money, then what you do must compensate for the lack of spending power. With luck, you won't even miss that spending power after a time and will actually wonder why on earth you were sucked into the system in the first place.

Portfolio living

Now, if you are going to downshift, one of the advantages is that you don't have to do one single job. You can do a variety. My wife and I between us teach adult education classes, train employees in industry, translate, write fiction, non-fiction and press releases, work for a relocation agency and give talks to groups. On top of that, we have to do a variety of other supporting activities to sustain our money-making work, such as book-keeping, typing and sending the annual accounts to the tax man. I am sure that if we wanted to, we could turn a lot of these tasks over to specialists and then devote our time to the most lucrative aspects of what we do. However, that would be missing the point. We are, in a way, self-sufficient when it comes to our money-making activities and recognise that doing such a wide variety of activities is much more interesting than having a single job.

In his book *The Age of Unreason*, Charles Handy uses the phrase "portfolio living" to describe a working life that is made up of a variety of different types of work. Of course, there are many people (cleaning ladies, for example) who have been doing this sort of thing for years and wouldn't even think of calling themselves portfolio workers. It is still a useful idea, though.

There is no reason why you couldn't come up with a variety of different activities that you could undertake in order to create a livelihood. In fact, if you look through your local newspaper, there are probably as many jobs for part-timers as there are for full-time workers. Part-timers offer their employers the ability to staff their businesses flexibly so that they can cover their busiest periods.

Similarly, as many businesses "stick to their core business", there is an increasing amount of work that they farm out to external contractors. Some of this work might not be enough to keep you going on its own, but, in combination with other activities, could help you towards putting together your own portfolio lifestyle.

Your house as your income

If you have owned your own house for any length of time, it is likely that it will be worth much more than you paid for it. On the downside, you might also have an enormous mortgage that you have to service though all your hard work.

Moving to a cheaper house, thereby reducing your outgoings will also have the effect of reducing the amount that you now have to earn in order to pay for your housing costs. Housing in some parts of the country has become so expensive that you might find that you could move to a similar house in another part of the country and actually be able to pocket a profit *and* get rid of the mortgage.

Not everyone wants to move, however, and you should also not overlook the fact that your house could be a valuable source of income, as well as providing you with working space should you so need it.

If you have the space in your house, and think you could stand sharing it with someone else, you might find renting out a room is a good way of bringing in income. If you live in London or a part of the country where rental accommodation is in short supply – such as a university town – this can be highly lucrative. You may find that contractors in your area only need accommodation from Monday to Thursday as they return home at weekends. This might be a good way of having an income during the week, but leaving you without the hassle of having a lodger cluttering up your kitchen and your family life at weekends. A self-contained area is perhaps best and renting out space can provide you with a degree of security and even companionship. Not only that, but under the Government's rent-a-room scheme, there is a valuable tax-free allowance for this.

However, you might find that the loss of privacy is too much for you to bear. In fact, you are essentially inviting a stranger into your house – there are occasional horror stories of the lodger who robs the landlord blind. There is also the possibility that conflicts could arise with your work and your family.

As with any home-based business there are also set-up costs: bed linen, alterations, furnishings and advertising as well as possible difficulties with your mortgage and domestic insurance.

However, using your home as the base for your business has many advantages to it. The cost and time involved in travelling to work are greatly reduced. You can also claim the cost of heating and lighting that part of your home you use for your work against tax. You can fit your working day around other commitments and decide how much work you are going to do. It is also a very cheap way of having business premises. Just find out how much it would cost to rent an office or a small industrial unit, let alone pay rates on them.

There are also, of course, disadvantages. Sometimes it becomes harder to separate out work from the other activities in your life, so you find that it is difficult to shut the study door. You may end up working longer hours than you did before as there is always a form to fill in, or a VAT return to complete or some other little job that needs addressing. You also need to make sure that there are no restrictions on using your house for business purposes. Normally this will depend on the type of business you run. If you're selling a typing service, you'll probably be fine. On the other hand, your local authority will look less kindly upon you if you want to turn your suburban garden into a small limestone quarry. You may also find your personal life intruding into your working life.

You may find your personal life intruding into your working life.

Working for yourself

If you decide that you want to work for yourself, it is a good idea to draw up a business plan. Check out your local library for information. You also might be able to get help from your local Business Link. It might surprise you, but your local bank is also a good resource – some of them supply business planning software and most of them are able to give you useful up-to-date leaflets and booklets. You might find writing a business plan a bit of a drag, but apparently a new business with a business plan is more likely to succeed than one without and is also likely to be more profitable. Even if it is a chore, it does help you to concentrate your mind on your business idea. You may find that there are courses on starting your own business in your area. Often these are free of charge.

Being self-employed also brings with it certain respon-sibilities. If you are currently employed, your employer probably takes care of all those nasty little things like tax, National Insurance and pension contributions. If you go self-employed, you are going to have to think about those for yourself. You may even have to think about VAT. You will certainly have to notify your home and contents insurer, your car insurer, your mortgage holder and possi-bly your local authority about your change in status and the use of your house for business purposes.

No matter how small your business, you are also going to have to ensure that you give the appearance of being profes-sional. It is no longer the case that anyone working from their home is viewed as being a bit dodgy. Tens if not hundreds of thousands of people do so nowadays. However, you do want your customers and potential customers to see you as being professional and efficient, whether you are teaching remedial English to young children or giving advice on mergers and acquisitions. You will probably need the kind of equipment and materials that give the impres-sion of a good solid business – a fax, a telephone answering machine, a proper invoicing system, letter-headed paper, an e-mail address, and perhaps even a dedicated phone number so that your customers are not greeted by your three-year old who insists on singing eight verses of Jingle Bells, no matter what season it is.

A few words of caution

Lastly, do not throw yourself into anything before you have thought about it. Both moving house and changing your job are fraught with difficulties.

Moving house is an expensive business. If you really like both the house and the area where you live, then there seems little point in giving it up for something else.

Working for yourself also sounds like an enormously attractive proposition, but the proportion of small businesses that fail each year is in the region of 30%. Also, one of the problems of working for yourself is that you are expected to be "successful". That success might have to come at the expense of everything you want from downshifting – the idea of a quieter, more reflective, more relaxed and more pleasant life.

Chapter 7

Be Frugal Not Stingy

My first rule of consumerism is never to buy anything you can't make your children carry.

Bill Bryson

One of the easiest ways to downshift is to stop spending your own money and to rely on other people to cough up on your behalf. After all, others have done this before you. Queen Elizabeth the First, a canny lady if ever there was one, spent a large part of her time moving around her kingdom, accompanied by a massive entourage of servants, body-guards, courtiers and assorted hangers-on. She would descend unannounced on the local gentry, who would then be forced to accommodate the Queen and her vast retinue.

You could do the twenty-first century equivalent. Many of us know people from all over the country – even from across the world. It wouldn't be too difficult to sponge off a number of friends throughout the year – eating their food, relishing their central heating and contributing nothing to their household bills.

Downshifting, however, does *not* mean that you should no longer part with your money. Nobody likes the kind of person who never buys a round or who is always scrounging off other people. I suspect the Earl of Scunthorpe, or wherever, upon seeing the Virgin Queen looming over the horizon, would feel his heart sink to his boots at the thought of how much she was about to cost him. If you did the same thing as the monarch, you'd soon run out of friends.

If you don't fancy free-loading, you could always go off and live in a yurt or a hut or a tepee somewhere. You could live off the land, capturing wild animals or picking berries from the hedgerows. You would truly be living at one with nature.

Henry Thoreau, the great nineteenth century down-shifter, did pretty much that. He went off to live in the woods, getting close to nature, eschewing the conveniences of his age with a cheerful disdain. However, I am reliably informed that every now and again his mates used to come round and take him off to civilisation for a few good nights out, a comfortable bed, hot baths and food. Not only that, but he was only thirty years old, probably didn't suffer too much from a bad back or arthritis and made money from doing it by writing a book called *Walden* about his experiences.

You don't have to live like a beggar or a mountain man to live frugally. Nor does being frugal mean being stingy. Our parents did it without a second thought and their parents before them must look on our current spending habits in bewilderment.

Living frugally is also a relative idea. My idea of living frugally would be a life of riches beyond compare for most of the inhabitants of the planet. There are also plenty of other downshifters who would regard my income and lifestyle as positively luxurious; others would see me as scraping by. For the sake of understanding what "frugal" means, let's just define it as being "living within your means". By questioning every decision about what you buy, how you buy it and when you buy it, you can cut down enormously on your costs without being stingy.

There are some simple rules for living frugally. You might like to add some more of your own, but if you ignore any of these it's a slippery slope back to indebtedness, the grind of the office and a more complicated life. If you're married, you might also like to know that the most frequently reported cause of marital friction is due to financial problems; then again, you might not. These can easily be avoided if you follow these twelve rules.

Rule One

● *Don't take home anything you can't eat or put to practical use, unless it is going to bring you lasting pleasure.*

This is simple enough. As we have seen in Chapter 3, all too often we end up buying things for their own sake. If buying a picture to go over your mantelpiece will bring you pleasure for years to come, then buy it – if you can afford it.

If it's just a passing fad, then don't. The easiest way to test if something is a passing fad or not, is to go home and see how long you can manage without the article in question. If you find you can cope pretty well without it, then you'll probably agree it was a passing fad and you didn't really need it after all.

Rule Two

● *Buy in bulk only if you use in bulk.*

Buying in bulk can make considerable cost savings. However, it needs storage space and money to be able to make the purchase in the first place. For instance, it may well be cheaper to buy your lavatory paper in job lots of a gross. After all, you're going to use it all at some point. You'll also find that you might be able to shave a couple of pence off the price of a roll. However, if by buying it you merely clutter up the spare room and also have to charge it to a credit card you can't pay off, then there really is no saving. If you make genuine savings, then buy in bulk by all means, but never buy anything that you won't use.

"**. . . But it was a *bargain!*"**

Buying in bulk is also pointless if you are buying produce that has a limited life. If you need four apples, then buy four apples. What's the point in buying two dozen even if it brings down the unit cost? Apples go off.

Rule Three

● *Buy the best you can afford.*

Not everything that is expensive is necessarily of high quality. There are dozens of branded sweatshirts, trainers, jeans and so on whose quality can easily be matched elsewhere.

However, when you buy very cheap goods they are often shoddy. Shop for quality rather than quantity. Having three good-quality T-shirts is a better investment than having half-a-dozen of inferior quality that cost just as much. If you buy the best that you can sensibly and reasonably afford, you will find that most things will last for a long time.

Rule Four

- *Think before you throw anything out.*

I've examined getting rid of clutter in Chapter 5. If you're throwing something out, you may well have to replace it. Ask yourself if that's really what to do. Go back to Chapter 5 and see what you can do with things you no longer need.

Rule Five

- *Think before you spend.*

Often we buy things because they are more up-to-date than the version we have. There are some lovely things in the shops and it's very easy to think that the latest version of a stereo system is going to be a whole lot better than an older one. It's not necessarily so. Sometimes we seem to spend money without giving it a passing thought or in a vain attempt to obtain something "extra special". According to the magazine *You and Your Wedding*, the average cost of a wedding is now £13,700. Given that so many weddings now end in divorce, it seems a lot to shell out for an even bet at a lifelong commitment. Perhaps couples think that the more they spend, the less likely it is that their marriage will end in divorce?

Rule Six

- *Is there a cheaper alternative?*

Although I recommend that you buy the best quality that you can afford, there are times when you should consider less expensive alternatives. If you fancy a meal out at Le Swanky, the latest riverside Bistro sensation, could you just as easily make do with steak pie and chips at the local pub? If you were going to have a take-away, why not rustle up a simple pasta dish instead? Do you really need that BMW, couldn't you get by with the old Ford?

Leisure goods and services are now the largest category of household expenditure. They tie for first place with the amount of money we spend on motoring and transport costs. It would seem that we are not prioritising where we spend our money.

In 1999, the average weekly expenditure on eating out was £5.20 per person per week – it was more in London. This is less than you might imagine, but if you add up the restaurant spending over the course of a year, it comes to over £250 – which would buy a truckload of groceries down at the supermarket.

Rule Seven

- *Is there an alternative to buying?*

So, you've decided not to buy the BMW and to plump for the old Ford instead. Well, perhaps you don't even need the old Ford. If you live in an area of the country that actually has public transport, you could use that instead. There are other possible alternatives to stumping up the money. If you're not much of a cook and are only ever going to make a cake on one occasion, there's little point in buying a food-processor. Why not borrow one instead? You can also hire tools, cars and any other item that you might not need to use on a regular basis. There are also alternatives to spending real money, which I will deal with later in this chapter.

Rule Eight

● *Buy fresh food in season.*

Rhubarb, potatoes and cabbage may be in season more or less all year round, but if you buy plums in January, they will be imported and consequently more expensive. Get yourself a chart of what British produce is available at what time of the year. Don't forget that if you buy cabbages, cauliflowers, "old" potatoes, Swedes and turnips, rather than more exotic produce, you can save a small fortune.

If you can, buy your fresh goods as direct from the source as possible. If you buy South African pears, for instance, you will be paying for all sorts of additional costs including transporting the pears, storage, distribution and so forth. If you buy your potatoes directly from the farm where they are grown, you are saving most of these costs.

Rule Nine

● *Buy consumer goods out-of-season.*

If you begin to get more with your money management, you will soon find that there are huge bargains to be had by buying your consumer goods at the wrong time of the year. This is at its most obvious in clothes shops, which sell their goods on a seasonal basis. If you buy your T-shirt after the summer has been and gone, you might well find it costs you less. A winter coat bought at the height of the mid-summer heat may also prove to be a bargain.

Start looking for other opportunities to buy out-of-season. If you are in the habit of sending Christmas cards, you will find that you can pick up Christmas cards and wrapping paper in the January sales at a fraction of the price they were just a fortnight earlier. Similarly, buy your barbecue or lawn-mower at the end of summer, when they're trying to shift these kinds of things off the shop floor.

Rule Ten

● *Make it yourself.*

It's a bit of an old-fashioned notion, but there are certain things that you can make for yourself. You don't have to be a brilliant craftsperson to make some of the things that you currently buy. Making greetings cards, for instance, requires very little skill. All you need is some card, a rubber stamp, an ink pad and a brightly-coloured pen and you're away.

Do-it-yourself has become one of the boom areas of the retail sector over the past couple of decades. You don't have to limit yourself to a bit of wall-papering. There are all sorts of crafts that you can indulge in that will save you money in the long run as well as providing you with a fun way to relax.

Rule Eleven

● *Grow it yourself.*

If you're old enough to remember the television series *The Good Life*, you will recall that Tom and Barbara Good dropped out of the rat race and attempted to become self-sufficient. They turned their suburban garden over to vegetable plots and pig pens. You don't have to do the same, but you might like to consider growing one or two things for your own consumption. You can make small savings this way and you can also boast that you grew it yourself. If you live in a flat, and only have a window box, you can always grow a few herbs. Hey, you could even grow some cress on the window-sill just like you did at primary school.

If you do have enough land to turn some over to production, you could keep a few laying chickens, which isn't exactly like laying the eggs yourself but it's the closest you're going to get.

Rule Twelve

- *Pay cash.*

If you're really good with your money, and pay off your credit card bill every month, you can ignore this, but only to an extent. The advantage of paying cash is that you can actually see how much money you are spending. This makes you more aware of what you are doing. There is also a further added advantage. If you pay cash, you can quite often negotiate a discount. Credit card companies charge shops a percentage of the transaction. Say you buy something for £100 and pay with the credit card, it is highly likely that the shop will have to part with at least £3 of that to the credit card company. You can, without looking to drive a hard bargain, always ask if the shop would be willing to knock off the cost of a credit card transaction if you pay cash. Many small traders also like cash and will offer to reduce the cost of a particular job if you pay them in real money. Unfortunately, this could well be because they are not declaring the income and are therefore avoiding VAT and tax. This is illegal.

Alternatives to money

So far, we have dealt purely in being frugal with money. Eking out your reduced income is important and there is one way in which you can do so without money, by finding alternatives to your usual currency.

Look at the money in your purse or wallet. I found a ten pound note in mine – just one unfortunately, but that's downshifting for you. It has a picture of the Queen on one side and one of Charles Darwin on the other. It also has all sorts of hallmarks, strips of metal and a washed-out colour look to it. I wouldn't go so far as to say it looks ugly, but frankly, it doesn't look like much. Somehow, it looks like proper money to me, not like the Toy Town stuff you get when you're abroad. The amazing thing with it is that for some reason the local shop will take it in exchange for groceries or books or stamps – despite the fact it's just a piece of paper.

The reason why my local shop will accept it is because we are all agreed that these pieces of paper mean something, that they have some value. It means that I can hand over a certain number of notes and coins in exchange for certain goods and services. The reason why foreign money looks like it's sneaked out of the toy box is that we are not used to handling it. Live in a country for any time and the currency becomes just as real as our own. Funny that.

Years ago, before the Queen and Charles Darwin started sneaking into wallets and purses all over the country (and then out again quicker than we ever thought they could), we used a system called barter. Barter, as you probably already know, is a series of ways of swapping things. It's just like the old kids' television programme *Swap Shop*, but without the inconvenience and doubtful pleasure of having Noel Edmonds and Keith Chegwin hovering around you trying to close the deal. So back in the old days, if I wanted a couple of sheep, you might offer me a smart axe in exchange.

It might be a bit rough and ready, but why can't you still offer goods and services that you possess in exchange for goods and services you do not? You have an old car, but you don't have a dining-table. You can teach someone French, but problems with your back mean that you have difficulty gardening.

But barter is a limited system. What happens if I don't want the axe? I've already got one, but I do need a hoe. I've either got to take the axe in the hope I'll find someone with a hoe who wants an axe, or I have to hang onto the sheep in the hope that I'll find someone with a hoe who wants a couple of sheep.

The same difficulty holds true today. If you can't find someone willing to take your fifteen year old Ford Fiesta off your hands in exchange for a dining table or a gardener keen to holiday in Brittany, it's a very limiting system. Cash makes everything easier, because you convert your car into cash (by selling it) and then use the cash to buy a dining table. Similarly, the money you get from teaching French can pay someone to work in your garden.

However, there are realistic alternatives to proper money as we know it. All over the country, there are schemes springing up where the pound sterling is not the currency of choice. One of the most popular of these schemes is called LETS and it is very likely that there is one near you.

LETS stands for Local Exchange Trading Systems. At the time of writing, there are over 450 of them and there are more starting every week. Essentially, the system is just the same as money. You provide an item or a service and you get paid for it, but instead of receiving normal currency you are paid in the unit of the local group. The names of the various currencies differ from group to group. In Ulverston in Cumbria, the unit of currency is named the Hoad after their local landmark, a replica of the Eddystone Lighthouse. Warminster goes for Links. Totnes has Acorns.

Each LETS group is entirely autonomous and, unless there is some kind of a local deal, units of currency are not transferable from one scheme to another. A group publishes a directory of members, each of whom lists the skills that he or she can offer. Members are encouraged to think beyond the obvious skills that they sell professionally, and to think about straightforward, helpful things that they can do such as simple DIY or gardening, or even waiting in for the washing-machine repair man. Members also advertise their wants and these vary enormously. My local group has wants that include putting up some shelves, help with setting up a permaculture allotment, some reiki healing and logs for a wood-burning stove.

There are several advantages to using the LETS scheme over using money. The first is that it doesn't involve money. If you have no money, it is an excellent way of sourcing the goods and services that you need. The scheme works no matter how little cash you have.

Secondly, a unit of currency banked under the LETS scheme does not attract interest. This means that if you are in debt, you are indebted to the scheme and not to a bank. You do not have to pay "interest" on your unit of currency and any real money that you save by swapping units of time instead of hard cash can be invested, thereby making you more money.

Thirdly, and especially if you live in a rural community, you will often be aware of how much money actually leaves the area. Buy from a big supermarket, a national chain of filling stations, burger bar or national department store and, aside from a small proportion going on local salaries, all the rest is siphoned back to head office, which could be at the other end of the country, or indeed thousands of miles across the sea. LETS actually keeps "money", goods and services in the area, so it doesn't simply appear as profit in the balance sheets of some multi-national corporation.

Fourthly, it is an invaluable way of creating a bit of community spirit. It enables you to meet people and to do business with them in the most co-operative way imaginable. Newcomers to LETS schemes are often worried about being ripped off by unscrupulous members who will join their LETS scheme, run up a whole load of debts and then leave the scheme without settling them. In practice, this very rarely happens, although some members are better at catching up on their debts than others. In terms of bad debts, the group actually takes the risk on behalf of the individual. If there are a hundred members of a LETS scheme and someone runs up a debt of 200 units, then that's only two units each. On the other hand, if you do a job for a company that then reneges on its debt or goes bust, you could lose the whole of your fee.

However, be warned. There are certain tax implications, although I am assured that the tax authorities give LETS traders "fair" treatment. If you are in receipt of a state benefit, you need to clarify the situation with your local benefits office.

If you are now richer in time than you are in money, LETS schemes are an excellent way of bringing a few touches of comfort to your life.

So, what now?

If you evaluate every purchase you make, you stand a much better chance of living within your means. If you don't like the rules I laid out earlier, perhaps you would find it easier to copy out the following onto a piece of card and stick it in your wallet or purse, right next to your credit card.

- Is it a necessity?
- Is it the best possible buy?

- Will it depreciate rapidly?
- Will it cost a lot to maintain?
- Am I buying this to fill some other gap in my life?
- What do I have to go without if I am going to buy this and live within my means?
- Why can't I wait 24 hours before I decide to buy?

Who knows, it might save you a fortune.

Chapter 8:

Do I Have to Go Green to Downshift?

We are living beyond our means. As a people we have developed a life style that is draining the earth of its priceless and irreplaceable resources without regard for the future of our children and people all around the world.

Margaret Mead

There often seems a big correlation between downshifting and the ecology movement, but do you really have to go green to downshift?

The quick answer is "no". You do not suddenly have to become green in order to be a downshifter. Downshifting is not an absolute. Downshifting is about arranging your priorities to suit yourself and your family. It does not mean a sudden and wholesale conversion from being the world's most wasteful person to being the kind of tyrant who goes around tut-tutting at anyone who buys a burger in a polystyrene box or who forgets to switch their engine off at the traffic lights.

One of the huge advantages of downshifting is that it does tend to give you a greener lifestyle. And if you have a greener lifestyle, then you are not damaging the planet as much as you were before. Some downshifters do a great deal more towards "going green" than others; harnessing wind and solar power in order to generate their own electricity, getting rid of their cars altogether and turning over whatever land they own to the cultivation of fruit and vegetables.

We all do some kind of damage to the environment, no matter how green we claim to be. It's almost impossible not to. The trendy little phrase for the amount of damage each one of us causes is the "ecological footprint", which is a wonderful term. Ecologists would argue that we have a responsibility to make our ecological footprint as small as possible. In fact, you don't have to be an ecologist to think we have that kind of responsibility; it seems a pretty obvious thing to do, really.

The largest ecological footprints on the planet belong to the Americans. What the Americans do today, we tend to do tomorrow. If we look at the United States of America as being the direction in which we are all heading, then we have good reason to fear for the planet. The ecological footprint of an American citizen is enormous. It is an elephant's ecological footprint compared to the mouse-size ones in developing countries. Although the United States only has 5% of the world's population, it consumes 30% of the world's resources. The amount of energy used by one American is the equivalent of that used by 168 Bangladeshis or 531 Ethiopians. A person living in the United States of America causes approximately one hundred times more damage to the global environment than a person living in a poor country.

If we are headed the way of America, then perhaps we need to take stock of a few statistics about the country's attitude to energy and waste. Unless we take positive steps, we could end up in the same boat. After all, we are one of the wealthiest countries in the world and consumption of energy is highest amongst the wealthiest countries. At the moment, Europeans as a whole produce less than half the waste per person than do the Americans. When you see how much the

Americans waste, there's no pride to be had from boasting that we waste only half as much – it's still a lot.

Waste Watch, experts on waste and recycling, estimate that in the UK we create around 25 million tonnes of household waste each year. As that means nothing, they go on to say that we produce enough waste to fill the Albert Hall every hour. And that's just domestic waste.

The average home wastes 60% of the energy it consumes. Our houses are so badly designed that the average UK house consumes something like ten times the amount of energy of state-of-the-art ecologically designed houses elsewhere in Europe.

Around one third of the miles that we drive by car each year are between home and work. We tend to be quite proud of our high mileages. A high mileage equals frenetic activity, equals a busy person. If I'm doing a lot of miles I must be important. High mileage becomes yet another shield from the reality of what we are doing to our environment. In 1950, the average Briton was quite content to travel about five miles a day. Now he or she will travel 28 miles. And we're not any more productive. What is worse is that our current 28 miles is predicted to double by the year 2025. Similarly, in 1971 around 80% of all seven and eight year olds walked to school; now virtually none does. You only need to drive at rush hour during school holidays to see how obviously fewer cars there are on the road.

Two thirds of our specially refined drinking water is used to flush lavatories or to wash clothes or dishes. It's yet another waste of a valuable resource. The thing about downshifting is that it asks you to re-think your role as a consumer. If you don't really want to think of yourself as a knit-your-own-tofu vegan, or think that sandals are the least attractive footwear of all time, then you can always tell yourself that the real reason why you have to stop being so wasteful as a downshifter is not to save the planet, but in order to save your own money. Saving the planet, or at least helping to conserve some of its resources, is a useful by-product. We are not concerned here with the kind of larger political issues concerning the environment, but with the smaller steps that you begin to take almost automatically as a downshifter.

Saving on Fuel

Let's give a few examples. Suppose, for the sake of argument, that you want to save money on your electricity bill. If you're earning a fortune, then some of the tiny steps you can take to cut down on electricity consumption will seem like penny-pinching. If you're living on a tighter budget, which is what you will more than likely have to do if you downshift, then a sum of money as small as ten pounds can take on a significance that might be laughable to other people. However, if you own a television set that is operated by a remote control, ten pounds is what it will cost you to leave the set in the "stand-by" position. When you switch off your television using the remote control, it does not switch off the set properly and the TV will still consume a small amount of electricity. If, as many people do, you have a couple of television sets, then you can save £20 per year by doing this.

Not only are you saving £20, but you are also doing a tiny little bit towards reducing the consumption of electricity and, consequently, helping to cut down on global warming. Now, saving £20 and having a tiny effect on global warming are not much in themselves, but imagine if every household in the country were to start doing it.

Similarly, if you are downshifting, you will probably look to re-discover some of those great skills that our parents and grand-parents trotted out all the time, but that we take for granted. When you are working all the hours God sends, cooking becomes a chore and you begin to rely on take-aways and restaurants not as some kind of treat, but as part of your way of life.

Re-discovering the joy of cooking is an integral part of downshifting. Anyone who can persuade you for one moment that shop-bought cakes, bread or puddings (apart from one or two rare cases) taste better than those made at home has ruined their palate with junk food.

Cooking does take energy and not just your own. If you're baking a cake or a loaf of bread, the oven needs to be heated. Cooking several cakes or loaves at once is a much more cost-effective way of cooking.

There is also a whole range of steps that you can take to reduce your energy bill before you even think about batch cooking and switching off your TV properly.

The traditional British home is poorly insulated, although we are getting better at it each year and new houses face more stringent regulations. Insulating your home as best you can is a vital way of conserving energy. Draught-excluders, loft insulation, double-glazing (or at least well-fitted windows), a lagged hot water tank and cavity-wall insulation are all effective ways of reducing your fuel bills. Fitting double-glazing can be very expensive and is likely to take some time to pay itself back, but cheaper measures such as fitting carpets and having good thick curtains at your window and drawing them at dusk are simple and effective.

Similarly, if you reduce the setting on your heating thermostat by just one degree centigrade, you can knock at least 5% off your annual fuel bill. Fitting thermostats to radiators, especially in rooms that you rarely use, can also reduce your spending on fuel. Sitting around in shirt sleeves in winter, with the thermostat turned up on full is not nearly as cost-effective as putting on an extra jumper. Other measures, such as showering rather than bathing, will also reduce your fuel costs, as well as using far less water. You will probably find that the local council or information centre has plenty of information on lowering your fuel bills. You can also contact the Energy Efficiency Office for much more detailed information. Even batteries are a form of fuel. If you've got plenty of gadgets around the house that use batteries, think about getting a battery recharger, or a mains unit.

Now, I suggest all these things in the name of saving you money. You will, of course, have twigged that as well as saving you money these kinds of actions will also have the knock-on effect of conserving energy in general, which has to be good for the environment. It cuts down on CO_2 emissions and global warming. You may even be eligible for some form of grant from your local authority.

There is a host of little steps that you can take in order to heat and light your home effectively and efficiently. Taking these little steps means that you are now becoming part of a virtuous circle. Whereas, before, your hectic lifestyle demanded easy, quick solutions to enable your life to run smoothly, you now have the time to take stock of what you are doing.

Transport Costs

There are other small savings you can make that also have a great knock-on effect. I am lucky in that I live next door to a farm. A sack of potatoes bought from my neighbour is a fraction of the price of a similar quantity bought over the weeks at the local supermarket. My motivation in buying his spuds is not to save the environment, but to cut down on my shopping bill. However, unlike the potatoes in my supermarket, these potatoes have travelled hardly any distance at all. I have saved the cost and damage to the environment of transporting potatoes from the farm to the depot and then to the supermarket and my journey to the supermarket. By buying locally, I've also ensured that my money is circulating locally. Had I visited the supermarket, most of what I would have paid would have ended up lining the pockets of someone in a completely different part of the country.

The same is true with personal transport. We all need to get to different places for our work or to see our friends and families. If we drive five hundred miles on our own to see our families in a car that only does 20 miles to the gallon, then we are causing more ecological damage than if we take the train. Owning any form of transport involves some kind of waste and use of energy. Even if you own a bicycle you have to be aware that making the bicycle was part of an industrial process involving raw materials, man-made materials, fuel, water and so forth. However, once you are using it, it has a very limited impact on the environment – much less than a car, or even a train. Of course, walking has the smallest ecological impact of all; although, if we walk along rural footpaths, we are in danger of eroding hillsides and natural habitats.

When we live a hectic lifestyle, we climb into the car to pop down to the corner shop for a loaf of bread. If we have more time, we can either walk or cycle. We can even cut out going to the shop for a loaf and bake our own bread.

It is often easiest to make do without a car if you live in a city. You stand a much better chance of having a decent public transport system. You may be able to manage without a car by using a mixture of public transport, taxis, hire vehicles, a bicycle and your own two feet.

In the country, which is where many downshifters find themselves, going without a car is often a great deal harder. Even if you are lucky enough to have a local train or bus service, you may well find that the service is infrequent. Trains and buses also have an annoying habit of not going exactly where you want them to go or, if they do, they do so at a time that is of no practical use to you.

Faced with this kind of situation, some downshifters are prepared to change the rhythm of their lives to that of the local transport network. However, if you examine a few rural timetables, you might find that idea a little intimidating and restricting.

In that case, you will almost certainly decide that you need a car. Running a car, even an older one, is an expensive business. In an attempt to get us into "greener" cars, the government has already introduced a cheaper road fund licence for smaller capacity engines and is set to take this idea several steps further. If you do decide that your lifestyle is such that you need a car, then you can save a great deal of money by buying second-hand. Simply driving a new car off the forecourt wipes several thousand pounds off the value. Also, if you buy a used car, you are in effect "reusing" something that someone no longer wants. You should ask yourself if you really need that souped-up coupé that does 20 miles to the gallon or if you shouldn't be looking towards something with a smaller engine that is a little more economical. With the price of petrol on a never-ending upward spiral, you will not only be saving a fortune in fuel costs, but also being kinder to the environment.

In the kitchen

If you are going to spend more time in the kitchen preparing food and making good meals where once you would send out for a take-away, you are inevitably going to produce some kitchen waste. You are not necessarily going to produce more waste than the person living out of the foil and cardboard containers from the local take-away, however. But the amount of waste we accumulate in our kitchens is quite terrifying.

For a start, there's all that packaging. We spend a fortune on the wrapping, boxes and labels that protect our produce. We may not have got as bad as the United States, but even so it's pretty worrying. It would appear that of the ninety million tonnes of waste we produce each year, two thirds of it goes into the ground. To risk sounding like a bad pun, this is an appalling waste. We can all improve what we do at home to minimise this waste.

The first thing to do is to re-use carrier bags whenever you can. In fact, if you get really well organised, you can get hold of better-quality plastic bags and keep them for quite some time. Then, you should try to make sure that you buy things that have less packaging. It's often quite hard to do this with new shirts, for instance, which come with more plastic, cardboard and pins than actual shirt. On the other hand, if you buy your fruit and vegetables loose, then you are saving on the packaging costs. Loose fruit and vegetables are also generally much less expensive than the packaged versions, so yet again, you are saving money and acting "green", without really having to give it too much thought.

If there is a good recycling scheme in your area, then you should try to use some kind of method of sorting out bottles, paper, tins and plastics. Most local authorities are getting much better at providing places for you to take your waste. However, if you have to make a special journey to the bottle bank, think about the damage you are doing to the environment in doing so. Tie it in with another trip.

It's quite amazing how much paper you can collect over time. Every morning's post brings with it all sorts of unsolicited mail. I am regularly offered credit cards I don't want and bank loans I could never afford. Some of the unsolicited mail you will receive will be sent because your name is on a mailing list. If you really don't want to receive this kind of post, ask for your name to be removed from the list. Details of how to do this are in the Appendix.

If you get some kind of a circular letter, you will often find that it is blank on the reverse. Try to use it as scrap paper. Open large envelopes carefully; they are enormously useful in a filing cabinet as they are far cheaper than proper stationery wallets. Again, the downshifter's philosophy comes through – you have saved on the time it would take to shop for proper stationery, you've saved the cost of the stationery and it is good for the environment.

Newspapers also tend to pile up. I'm certainly not advocating going without a daily newspaper if it gives you pleasure. One of the great advantages of downshifting is that it gives you the time to read, do the crossword and to become better informed about domestic and international affairs. If you don't want the expense of a daily paper, you can always go to your local library to read one (preferably on foot or by bike). However, buy a daily newspaper and the amount of paper in your house soon stacks up. You can make fuel from the newspapers using a special compressing machine. You need to soak the paper before compressing it into briquettes. It's an inexpensive form of fuel, but the trouble is that you do need somewhere to do this as it can be quite messy and also a place for your damp briquettes to dry out.

You can also shred newspaper and tissues to go into your compost heap, but you shouldn't over-do it. If you've not got a compost bin and you have the space in your garden for one, then it is a great idea to get one. Although you probably couldn't put all of your newspaper into it, it will take an occasional layer. It will also take lawn clippings, potato peelings, carrot scrapings, left over food (best not to put meat in as it can attract vermin), apple cores, tea leaves, coffee grounds, egg shells, weeds, animal manure, clippings from evergreens, leaves, garden prunings, straw, hay and even hair off the cat, dog or your own head. Also, if you've ever wondered what to do with the dust from inside your vacuum cleaner – you can put that in as well. In fact a compost bin is a great place for any kind of organic waste.

Some people prefer to leave all their garden clippings and prunings in a pile, but a bin is a neater way of stacking it all up and will give better results, especially if, like me, you're not much of a gardener. If you've ever seen the price of compost in the shops, you will see that it is a great way to save money and the resulting compost is good for your garden. Again, you're saving money and benefiting your environment.

Now, the other thing that compost does is to re-use waste in a truly sensible fashion. There is an enormous knock-on effect for the environment. Apparently, around 30% of household waste is in the form of organic waste. Normally, this would simply go into land-fill sites. By composting, you are helping to save acres of the earth for something a little more useful, like growing vegetables or housing. The amount of rubbish you no longer put in your wheelie bin, dustbin or black bag is so great that many local councils periodically give away composting bins free of charge or sell them at an amazingly cheap price. It's in their interests to do so.

Lastly, don't forget that there are various organisations, especially charities, who often collect certain unwanted items. Milk bottle tops and stamps are two frequent choices. Find out if anyone near you collects anything like that. If they do, it's no great hardship to hang a couple of carrier bags on the back of the kitchen door and stick them in. You'll also be making friends with whoever comes to collect them.

A study or home office often tends to be the kind of room where people are loath to throw things way just in case they need them. If you've got any old laser or photo-copier cartridges lying around the place, there are many charities who collect them and sell them on to recycling companies. By getting rid of some clutter, you are both helping a charity and the environment.

If you can, try to recycle: newspapers and other kinds of paper; cans – tin and aluminium; bottle tops; glass; food scraps; batteries; plastics; egg cartons; clothing, bedding and other textiles; furniture; electrical appliances. Just by doing that, you are reducing your "ecological footprint" dramatically.

Some Rules of Thumb

There is no doubt that, if we take a more frugal approach to our everyday lives, being 'green' follows on in many ways. The important thing is that we break out of the vicious circle of working so ridiculously hard that our money goes on expensive gadgets and gimmicks and to sustain a life-style that, quite frankly, we don't want.

Instead, we need to get ourselves into a virtuous circle. If we have more time and energy to devote to things that really matter, we can also do our little bit to help the environment. It doesn't matter that we don't go the whole hog. Frankly, I am not going to give up central heating, my car, mains electricity and running water to go and squat in a rain-soaked field somewhere. I like my creature comforts and have got used to them. Nor am I going to turn my little garden into an allotment. For a start I'm not a gardener and what little space there is I want for sitting out in and having barbecues in the summer. I'm quite happy that we just grow a few herbs and that our pretty little apple tree gives us enough for a couple of pots of jam in the autumn.

However, what I do try to do, in common with most of the downshifters I talked to while researching this book, is to think about what I do in terms of its costs. Nearly always, if something is an expensive alternative it is also more damaging to the environment.

When you go to the shops to buy something, you should already be asking yourself if you need it or if there's a cheaper alternative. We've already looked at this in Chapter 3 when we looked at the idea of saving money. Buying less will also cut down on your packaging waste – there is a green knock-on effect. I also advocate borrowing things, if appropriate, as this too cuts down not only on your expense but also on the amount of energy and raw materials that goes into making that item in the first place. Although, if you do borrow things, you should be prepared to lend your own things in return – downshifting is not all one-way traffic.

If you buy something you should make sure that you do one of the following three things with it:

- Wear it out.
- Mend it.
- Use it up.

This kind of attitude to your possessions, clothes, food – in fact towards anything that you buy – will not only save you a fortune from the moment you start doing it, but will also contribute towards saving a great deal of wear and tear on our already over-stretched environment.

Chapter 9:

Is Downshifting for You?

I don't want to belong to any club that will accept me as a member.

Groucho Marx

The beauty of downshifting is that it is not an absolute. The multi-millionaire who moves to a smaller mansion is as much a downshifter as the factory worker who decides to give over his life to working on community projects.

There are also no rules to downshifting. You don't have to give up your car, your house, your hobbies or your friends. Nor does downshifting mean that you have to accept as gospel a whole series of principles. If you join an ecological organisation, for instance, you will probably be expected to agree broadly with their agenda (although you would also be expected to contribute to it). If you downshift, you can create a whole agenda for yourself. It's not like joining a political party where you have to toe the party line or else they throw you out. You can do what you like. And that's real freedom.

Because of this vagueness, you can't apply the kind of economic measurement that you can to other social trends. To date, the marketing men have not yet worked out how they can make any real money from downshifting. Indeed, if you were to read the reviews of Juliet Schor's book, *The Overworked American*, in which she discusses the way in which America has become crazy for long hours and money, you would find that they were very positive indeed – save for the review by the *Wall Street Journal*. You can make your own guess as to whether or not this was for social and political reasons.

Inevitably, when we think of downshifters, our minds turn to the good-lifers of the 1970s who dropped out of the rat race and went off to live on a smallholding in Wales with seven sheep and a milk cow. Times were different then. If you were a professional person, you would probably have to work as an employee of a company or large public organisation. The idea, especially for a man, of working part-time would have been considered very strange. You either stayed in the system full-time or you fell out of it completely.

Times have changed. Companies and government organisations have shed a lot of staff over the past decade or so and they are used to replacing that expertise by buying in part-time or temporary experts from outside the organisation. You can downshift by holding on to some of the skills you have developed over the years and using them commercially. At the same time, you are banishing from your life some of the elements that you find too much – the travel, office politics, crazy hours, business suits, or whatever.

I suppose that if you want to define what downshifting is, you have to think of it in terms of being less of one thing and more of another. Downshifting is concerned with being less of a slave to the demands of work and the stresses and pace of modern life. It is more to do with determining what you actually want from life and ensuring that you achieve it. It's about getting your own personal life/work balance the way you want it.

Reality vs. illusion

Downshifting is also about facing up to the reality of your situation. If the only reason you joined the company was so that you could rise to become Managing Director, yet others are being promoted above your head, then why continue in the job? You might simply want to change jobs, but downshifting gives you an additional choice.

Some of us are often lured by the extravagant lifestyles that we see paraded on our television screens into wondering what life would be like if we had more money than we could ever dream of. Ask yourself some questions.

Do you really need a bathroom for every bedroom in the house? Do you really need to go to the Bahamas to recharge your batteries when you've never even visited the National Trust property on the other side of town? Do you really need that £28,000 off-roader just to run the kids to school or pick up the supermarket shopping?

We've all been seduced into thinking that more equals better. This simply can't be the case. As Spock would say, it isn't logical. If we can only improve our lives by having more, then we can never improve our lives. Owning the next item on our list of must-haves means that we must now progress to the next and the next one and so on ad infinitum. If we can only be happy by owning more than we already have, then we can never be happy. It's glaringly obvious, really. *Whoever's got the most toys in the graveyard hasn't necessarily won.*

We think that being rich will solve all of our problems. We spend millions of pounds every week on the National Lottery, which is the biggest purveyor of the dream of instant riches. Our conversations still include wild speculations about what we would do if we were to win some multi-million pound fortune.

Playing the lottery may seem like a bit of harmless fun, but it could also have some hidden dangers. For a start, there is no proof whatsoever that increased wealth brings increased happiness. In fact, making the simple equation wealth = happiness tends to distort the realities of our lives.

The reality is that we are very unlikely ever to be rich, but if we think about how wealthy we are compared to the vast majority of the world's people, then we probably possess wealth greatly in excess of what they can ever dream about themselves.

Playing the lottery is a fantasy activity. You only have to look at the odds of winning to see what a waste of money it is. If you buy a single £1 ticket, you stand one chance in 13,983,816 of winning the jackpot. If you express this as a decimal, you will find this reads as 0.0000000715. This is such a small number that you might as well say that your chances of winning are zero. Yes, I know you can only win if you have a ticket, but your chances are almost the same without.

Hoping to win an extreme fortune using methods that demand huge slices of good luck also means that you are in fact working on the basis of hope – that something over which you have no control is going to come to your rescue – rather than doing something practical about your situation. "Ah, but it's only a fiver a week," you say. True, but if you saved that fiver a week for thirty years, you would have £7,800 at the end of it, plus all the interest that the money will have accrued over the years. Well, it may not be the same as winning £7,800,000 on the lottery, but at least it's guaranteed and you also have some idea of what you can really do with that kind of sum.

In fact, your odds of achieving happiness are much greater if you downshift than if you play the lottery. There's no guarantee that you are going to be happier than before but, according to the Merck Family Fund, a US charity, 87% of people in America who choose to downshift describe themselves as happy with the changes that downshifting has brought to their lives. You don't have to be a mathematical genius to see that an 87% chance of happiness is much better odds than a lottery win.

What the Merck Family Fund also found was that the four main reasons for downshifting were so that people could enjoy a more balanced life, have more time in general, find a less stressful way of life and spend more time with their children.

However, be warned. Thirty-five per cent of the downshifters in the survey admitted that they did miss the extra income. The sooner we realise that all life is a trade-off between time and money the better. Only you can tell if having less money is worth it if it means having more time to spend with your family or to pursue other activities.

When you downshift, you have to look at your real current situation and not the imaginary one in which you might find yourself if only six of those forty-nine little balls would fall just right for you. Reality says that you must clear your debts, build up some savings and consider where you might live and the work you might do. If you are very lucky, you might already be in a position where you are financially independent – in which case the world is your oyster.

Others are not so lucky. Their decisions have perhaps been at least half made for them already. Major changes in circumstances often force people to look for radical solutions to their problems. If you suddenly realise that you are fifty years old, redundant and used to having an executive's salary, but that companies are only ever going to interview people under the age of forty, then you have some serious choices to make. If you've had a serious illness and can no longer do what you did before, you too are facing a difficult situation. You can either rail against the injustice of a system that scraps its experienced workers or the unfairness of your illness or you can turn that experience into something else more positive and use it to your advantage. Downshifting provides one way of addressing these kinds of problems.

Life is so often a series of ladders: school, college, work, greater responsibility; bed-sit, flat, semi-detached house, detached house. But if you don't feel comfortable with the conventions, you don't have to follow them. Basically, if you always do what you've always done, then you'll always get what you've always had. Thoreau, the great American downshifter of an earlier age, puts it in a nutshell: "Life is a journey, not a station". If you think that your life is stuck at the station and you want it to be a journey, then downshifting is one way of achieving it.

Another important aspect of downshifting is that it doesn't necessarily last for ever. A friend of ours who used to hold a very senior position in a large national company was becoming increasingly disillusioned with the way in which the ethos of the company was changing: "We used to be gentlemen and now we're sharks". He had no luck finding similar work elsewhere and the situation in his own company became so dire that eventually he left of his own free will and spent some time living a much less affluent lifestyle, with the occasional short-term contract, before finding that he was in demand for temporary work as an interim Managing Director for companies who were undergoing problems. In fact, far from downshifting, he and his family are enjoying an even better lifestyle than before. The pay-off is that, instead of dreading every minute of his work, he now loves it. He works just as hard as he did previously, but has a renewed vigour and energy that he probably wouldn't have had if he had stayed in his previous job.

Unsurprisingly, if your earnings are higher, you have a greater amount of choice and flexibility. Occupying a senior position in commerce, industry or the public sector gives people a good basis to take up part-time or contract-based work with a variety of organisations. You should also be able to make greater savings, and have property and other assets that are worth more than most of us own. There is no doubt that downshifting is easier when you have more capital behind you. However, there are many other part-time and contract-based jobs lower down the pay-chain that are yours for the taking if you know where to look for them.

All downshifters, regardless of their comparative incomes, are able to indulge themselves in a wider range of work than they might have done had they been in a "proper" job. Downshifting does not mean that you have to concentrate just on one particular kind of activity. Many downshifters have a series of activities that they undertake – some paid, some unpaid – that go to make up their lifestyle. In these cases, what they find is that the work they love doing – a craft for instance – does not bring in sufficient money of its own accord, so they have to do something else in order to "buy" the time to do what they enjoy doing the most. Strangely, instead of resenting the "real" work, some have found that they enjoy it so much that they are loath to give it up.

You can also consider that the time you have gained by not commuting to work could be put to good use. There are many things that you can do that are fulfilling, but do not count as "work" as we know it. Voluntary work, travel, reading, writing, studying, discovering something about your family history, pursuing hobbies, reducing your environmental impact – all these are realistic and achievable, if you are not hamstrung by a lunatic, long working week.

Children

There is no doubt that downshifting is easier without children. For a childless couple, who are both capable of earning money, the number of permutations of part-time or short-term work, freelancing and so forth is great. You are able to rely on one another without thinking too hard about the repercussions of your actions.

In the Merck Family Fund survey, more than half of the respondents stated that they had downshifted to spend more time with their children. Perhaps downshifting for the sake of the children is not as ridiculous as it might appear and shows that we realise how much damage we are doing to them. And we do have reason to be worried. According to the pressure group Mothers in Management, in a report entitled "Time Bomb – Why We Need To Change The Way We Work", twenty percent of children suffer from a stress-related health problem, simply as a result of Britain's "long hours culture" and the stresses of the 24-hour a day economy. In fact, stress now costs the National Health Service £2 billion per year. The stresses on children and parents as individuals and the resulting strains on the family as a whole can be very dangerous indeed.

A recent newspaper article showed how parents were becoming increasingly annoyed at some football teams who change the designs of their team strips too often, "forcing" the parents to buy the latest version for their children. There is an easy answer to this: you don't have to have the latest thing just because it's the latest thing. You are indulging your children and putting money into the pockets of profiteers. If a team keeps on doing this, the answer is not to buy the new shirts, *and* to stop supporting the team.

If your children are prepared to go without the latest crazes, then they might find that the extra time they have with you can bring about different kinds of rewards, including greater success at school.

The time to act is now

There is the old saying, "I've been too busy making a living to make any money". You could equally say, "I've been too busy making a living to have a life". So, if you don't really think you've got a proper life, why not do something about it? You have to make the decision to stop going round in circles.

There are many reasons why we don't get things done. We are always looking for excuses for why the windows haven't been repainted, the lawn mowed or granny visited. We tend to use lack of time or lack of money or lack of energy to explain away these little failures, but if we are to be really honest, we can add to the list a lack of application, fear of failure or simply not being quite sure what needs doing. We are in danger of applying the same delaying tactics to our decision-making.

If you think that downshifting is a realistic option for you, you need to start giving it some serious thought. It's worth using a basic five-point plan of the sort that is often bandied around on management courses.

Your five-point plan for dropping out

Everyone needs a plan and here's one way of coming up with one.

- First, you should know your strengths. You need to ask yourself if you have the right temperament, attitude and determination to live a simpler life.
- Secondly, you have to know your limitations. If you couldn't ever see yourself managing without six brand-new tailor-made suits every year, then perhaps you need to sort out your present situation in some other way. If you like the security of a monthly pay slip or the weekly pay packet, then downshifting by moving into an area of self-employment may also be difficult. However, limitations are not blocks and can often be easily overcome. If you would like to work for yourself, but think that without any book-keeping skills or computer know-how it would be difficult, then you have already defined your personal limitations and can put them right – in this case possibly by taking a

part-time course or reading books on the subject.

- Thirdly, you need to work out why you want to down-shift. At this stage, the old trick of ruling a line down the middle of a sheet of paper and writing the pros on one side and the cons on another is not a bad idea.

- Fourthly, you need to work out *when* you can achieve this. You must be realistic about your expected income, paying off your debts, your savings and all the other financial matters we have discussed in previous chapters.

- And fifthly, you need to establish *how* you can achieve this. If you need to save ten thousand pounds, for instance, then how are you going to do so? Will you be selling a car, your stamp collection or saving a hundred pounds a month for the best part of ten years?

Fools rush in

If you are serious about dropping out of the rat race and going for a simpler life, then one of the easiest ways of doing it is to go into work tomorrow and hand in your resignation. If there is lots of work at your current level in your particular field, then you're not risking a great deal. For most people, however, doing this would be the path to financial and personal ruin.

To begin with, you could start by asking yourself some fundamental questions. What is of real value to you? How do you define success? I suspect that for many of us the answers are not the kinds of things that society in general would have us believe in. Don't forget – you have to work out what is wrong with your life before you can decide what to do to put it right.

Whatever you define as success, you need drive and determination to make it happen. You need to have a common sense approach to creating realistic and achievable aims and objectives and you need to keep your eye on them, so that you know in which direction you are heading.

And within all this, you also need sound financial planning to take into account your personal overheads and living costs, your personal finances and, if you decide to start your own small business, that too will require its own financial planning.

Only you can determine the timescale for downshifting. It might be quite useful for you to have a set of aims and objectives. Aims are the overall goals that you have; objectives are the little steps that you need to take in order to meet those goals. So, for instance, if you decide that you would like to set up as a freelance book-keeper, then that is an aim. The objectives are all the things that you will have to do in order to get there – ordering stationery, registering for VAT, upgrading your computer, advertising and so forth. In other words, each leap that we take requires a set of little steps in order to get where we want to be going.

Planning our lives is important. No, life won't go smoothly. Planning your life will not mean that your life will go according to plan! But at least planning provides us with an idea of where we want to go. The two-thirds of adults who play the lottery each week are not planning their lives, they are merely clutching at straws. People who, instead of gambling their average £2.50 a week, put it into a savings account in order to boost their retirement pension are planning their lives.

Good luck!

It can be a little bit frightening to think that you are going to be the first to do something. Not all of us are cut out to be pioneers and pathfinders. It may be worth reminding yourself that if you downshift, you will not be the first person to do so. Jesus, Buddha, Thoreau, Gandhi, Tom and

Barbara Good, and countless others, have all done it before you. Nobody knows how many downshifters there are out there. The early retired, part-time workers, redundant managers, as well as those who have chosen to leave the rat race behind to pursue careers in the arts or the crafts, start their own small businesses or simply to have time to smell the roses – all of them are downshifters.

However, there is no doubt that it takes a little bit of courage to say that you are no longer going to be motivated by the external trappings of success or by what society generally expects from us.

If you decide that you do want to drop out – if you do decide that downshifting is for you – then you are not alone. You may end up with less money than you had before, but there is no way in which you will ever be poorer. After all, with planning and some luck, you will find that you have all the time, energy and oomph that the rat race is currently sucking out of you.

Remember – whatever epitaph you choose, the chances are that it will never, ever be, "I wish I'd spent more time at the office".

Appendix

If you've read this far, you are probably genuinely interested in the idea of changing the way in which you live. It's an important decision to make and one that will inevitably have a huge impact on the lives of you and your family. I think that the only person who can make that decision is you. However, it is useful to know of other sources of information.

There are various organisations that keep their information as up-to-date as they can and you might find some of their information useful. It is not an exhaustive list and I expect that there are organisations you know of that could also have been included. However, all of them deal with at least one aspect of the life of a downshifter – volunteering, conservation, teleworking, alternative technologies, education or community issues. Some of them will not be relevant to you, or you might think are plain silly. However, they do all provide a slightly different view of the world from the prevailing climate and are useful at least just for that.

If you are writing to any of them, don't forget to include a large stamped, addressed envelope – after all it helps to keep their costs down.

The Barataria Foundation

Keepers Cottage, Pitlandie, Luncarty, Perthshire, PH1 3HZ,
   UK
Telephone: 01738 582232
E-mail: ruth@barataria.org

Barataria was the name of the mythical kingdom given by
Don Quixote to his manservant Sancho Panza to govern.
Quixote expected Sancho Panza to make a real mess of it,
but he governed the kingdom well and wisely. The Barataria
Foundation is a Scottish charity that wants to inject the
same compassion and wisdom into everyday life. "The
Foundation believes that new solutions must be found
which protect our communities from the effects of global
change."

The British Franchise Association

Thames View, Newtown Road, Henley-on-Thames, Oxon,
   RG9 1HG, UK
Telephone: 01491 578049
Fax: 01491 573517
E-mail: mailroom@british-franchise.org.uk
Web: www.british-franchise.org.uk

A very useful resource if you are considering taking up a
franchise. Formed in the 1970s to ensure that franchising
in the United Kingdom developed ethically, the BFA
encourages good practice amongst members and acts as
an information service for would-be franchisees. Fran-
chisor members of the BFA have to prove that they are
financially viable, ethical and can successfully be franchised. It should be the first port of call for any would-be
franchisee.

British Trust for Conservation Volunteers (BTCV)

36 St Mary's Street, Wallingford, Oxfordshire, OX10 0EU,
  UK
Telephone: 01491 839766
Fax: 01491 839646
E-mail: information@btcv.org.uk
Web: www.btcv.org.uk

Every year over 4,000 people from all walks of life take part
in BTCV activities. The idea is to combine a holiday with a
conservation activity, such as hedge laying, coppicing, dry
stone walling, preventing sand dune erosion, improving
footpaths and managing wetlands. Most of their activity
holidays are in the UK, many in beautiful parts of the
country, such as Cumbria, the North York Moors, Cannock
Chase, the Forest of Bowland or the Pennines. There are
even opportunities to travel abroad and indulge in such
exotica as radio-tracking wolves in Slovakia.

Business Link Network Company

39 London Road, Newbury, Berks, RG14 1JL, UK
Telephone: 01635 572600
Fax: 01635 572601
E-mail: info@blnc.co.uk
Web: www.businesslink.co.uk

Business Link is a national network of local business advice
centres, which offer information and advice to new and established businesses. They can help in key areas such as marketing, sales, finance, export and general business development.
Many of them also run courses on starting your own business.
  They also run the Business Link Signpost Line, which will
point you in the direction of your local business link.
Telephone 0845 7567765.

Centre for Alternative Technology

Machynlleth, Powys, Wales, SY20 9AZ, UK
Telephone: 01654 702400
Fax: 01654 702782
E-mail: info@cat.org.uk
Web: www.cat.org.uk

CAT describes itself as "seven acres of environmental solutions to inspire, inform and entertain". They have on display all sorts of alternatives to traditional technologies, including wind, solar and water-based energy. They run courses, where you can study anything from blacksmithing to alternative funerals and learn how to build anything from a yurt to a detached house. You can even live in an eco-cabin to witness new technologies first hand. CAT also has a thriving mail-order business, from which you can buy books, plans, kits and smaller items of alternative technology. CAT run a membership scheme called the Alternative Technology Association, which, amongst other benefits, gives discounts on CAT publications.

Eco-logic Books

19 Maple Grove, Bath, BA2 3AF, UK
Telephone: 01225 484472
Fax: 01179 420164
E-mail: books@eco-logic.demon.co.uk
Web: www.ragmans.co.uk/eco-logic/eco-logic.html

Eco-logic Books' catalogue is a masterpiece in its own right. Each book is given a witty little description. Eco-logic cover gardening, smallholdings, wildlife, housing, community development, the economy, alternative technologies, alternative business and children's books. They also sell other items that fit with a greener life-style, including electric bicycles.

Ecology Building Society

18 Station Road, Cross Hills, Nr. Keighley, West Yorkshire,
   BD20 7EH, UK
Telephone: 0845 674 5566
Fax: 01535 636166
E-mail: info@ecology.co.uk
Web: www.ecology.co.uk

The Ecology Building Society states in its literature that it
"provides a means of finance for the purchase of properties
that give an ecological payback". They specialise in lending
money for houses that incorporate special energy-saving
features, derelict houses for rebuilding, back-to-backs, work-
shops, organic smallholdings and farms and homes for people who are involved in businesses with an ecological bias.
They often find themselves funding projects that the traditional lenders would not consider. They even have buy-to-let
mortgages, which allow prospective landlords to buy property for renovation before renting it out. They also have
several savings accounts, including a special charity account.

Education Otherwise

PO Box 7420, London, N9 9SG, UK
Telephone: 0870 730 0074
E-mail: enquiries@education-otherwise.org
Web: www.education-otherwise.org

"It shall be the duty of the parent of every child of compul-
sory school age to cause him or her to receive efficient
full-time education suitable to his/her age, aptitude and
ability (subject to any special educational needs he/she
might have) either by attendance at school or otherwise." So
runs Section 7 of the 1996 Education Act. Many people do
not know about the important last two words of the act "or

otherwise". In other words, you do not have to send your child to school. You can teach him or her at home.

Education Otherwise is an organisation that provides a network of support for parents who have decided, for a whole variety of reasons, to educate their children outside the mainstream.

Emerson College

Pixton, Hartfield Road, Forest Row, East Sussex, RH18 5JX, UK
Telephone: 01342 822238
Fax: 01342 826055
E-mail: info@emerson.org.uk
Web: www.emerson.org.uk

Emerson College is an adult education college which holds courses based on the works of Rudolf Steiner. They hold all sorts of courses, including puppetry, Shakespeare, Teaching English as a Foreign Language and Environment. There is also the opportunity to get away from it all for a spiritual retreat.

Energy Savings Trust

21 Dartmouth Street, London, SW1H 9BP, UK
Telephone: 020 7222 0101
Fax: 020 7654 2444
Web: www.est.org.uk

Contact the Energy Savings Trust and they will send you a pack which shows you exactly how much energy you can save around the home. Their booklets give advice on loft insulation, thermostats, boilers – in fact anything to do with saving energy in the home. If you telephone 0800 512 012, they will put you in touch with your local Energy Efficiency Advice Centre, who will be able to inform you if there are any local schemes available for subsidising the costs of improving the energy efficiency of your house.

Environment Agency

Rio House, Waterside Drive, Aztec West, Almondsbury,
　Bristol, BS32 4UD, UK
Telephone: 01454 624 400
Fax: 01454 624 409
Web: www.environment-agency.gov.uk

This is the government-funded organisation that aims to improve the quality of our air, land and water and to encourage conservation of natural resources. If you want to know more about the environment in your area, you can go to the Environment Agency's website and tap in your postcode. It will tell you about the condition of rivers, beaches and so forth where you live.

Environmental Transport Association

10 Church Street, Weybridge, Surrey, KT13 8RS, UK
Telephone: 01932 828 882
Fax: 01932 829 015
E-mail: info@eta.co.uk
Web: www.eta.co.uk

A green alternative to the major breakdown services, ETA offers a full service for drivers and motorcyclists as well as offering what they claim is the only cyclists' rescue service that is comparable with motorists' breakdown assurance. In addition to running their breakdown service, the ETA also campaign for a sustainable transport policy and that priority be given to the most environmentally friendly forms of transport. Every year they promote the ETA National Car Free Day.

Ethical Consumer Magazine

ECRA Publishing Ltd, Unit 21, 41 Old Birley Street,
    Manchester, M15 5RF, UK
Telephone: 0161 226 2929
Fax: 0161 226 6277
E-mail: ethicon@mcr1.poptel.org.uk
Web: www.ethicalconsumer.org

"Ethical Consumption put simply is buying things that are made ethically by companies that act ethically." The magazine investigates different products and companies in order to give readers an insight into which companies are behaving "ethically". Articles cover such issues as how far your vegetables have travelled or which computer companies are acting "green". A useful guide if you feel strongly about these kinds of things.

Ethical Investment Research Service

80-84 Bondway, London, SW8 1SF, UK
Telephone: 020 7840 5700
Fax: 020 7735 5323
E-mail: ethics@eiris.org
Web: www.eiris.org

If you are concerned that you don't want to invest in companies that have interests in areas that go against your principles, then EIRiS is able to help. If you feel strongly about the arms trade, tobacco, pollution of the environment, genetic engineering, pesticides, human rights or any similar concerns, EIRiS can identify companies who make their profits from these areas. There are various services they offer the small investor, from the supply of fact sheets to the screening of your portfolio.

Fair Shares

City Works, Alfred Street, Gloucester, GL1 4DF, UK
Telephone: 01452 541337
Fax: 01452 541352
E-mail: fairshares@cableinet.co.uk
Web: www.fairshares.org.uk

Based on the American concept of Time Dollars, Fair Shares is a charity that works to encourage people to volunteer for work in their local communities. Not dissimilar from the LETS scheme, it is about offering your skills, talents and aptitudes to the community in return for skills, talents and aptitudes that you might not possess. The principle behind the scheme is that, in the long run, it will increase community participation.

The Findhorn Foundation

The Park, Findhorn, Forres, IV36 3TZ, UK
Telephone: 01309 690311
E-mail: genoffice@findhorn.org
Web: www.findhorn.org

Perhaps the best-known fact about the Findhorn Foundation is that some of the people who live in the Findhorn community live in converted whisky vats. The foundation performs a number of functions, including encouraging the spiritual, social, economic and environmental aspects of life. They also run an enormous adult education programme with all sorts of different courses addressing spirituality, less well-known and eastern religions, dance, communication, permaculture, psychology, and even golf.

Global Action Plan

8 Fulwood Place, Gray's Inn, London, WC1V 6HG, UK
Telephone: 020 7405 5633
Fax: 020 7831 6244
E-mail: all@gapuk.demon.co.uk
Web: www.globalactionplan.org.uk

Global Action Plan believe that everyone can do their bit for the environment – you don't just have to be an environmental activist. They have four programmes of activities, which involve action at home, at work, at school and an initiative they call "small change", which is concerned with helping households in disadvantaged communities to use energy more efficiently, eat more healthily and to cut pollution. They believe that by educating people into small changes in their habits, such as not leaving the TV on standby, they can achieve larger changes.

Groundwork UK

85-87 Cornwall Street, Birmingham, B3 3BY, UK
Telephone: 0121 236 8565
Fax: 0121 236 7356
E-mail: info@groundwork.org.uk
Web: www.groundwork.org.uk

Groundwork UK has been running for about twenty years now. It is a network of not-for-profit companies who work to help local communities improve the environment in which they live. Local Groundworks co-operate with other businesses and local authorities to develop projects that will benefit both the local economy and the environment. They are heavily involved in tree-planting, the reclamation of derelict land, the creation of parks and recreation spaces and involving youngsters from local schools in the process. They publish several useful leaflets and a newsletter.

Henry Doubleday Research Association

Ryton Organic Gardens, Coventry, CV8 3LG, UK
Telephone: 024 76 303517
Fax: 024 76 639229
E-mail: enquiry@hdra.org.uk
Web: www.hdra.org.uk

HDRA is concerned with organic gardening. Membership gives you a quarterly magazine, discounts in HDRA's extensive organic gardening catalogue, the use of the reference library and discounts on courses and events held at Ryton. More importantly, it gives you access to organic gardening advice and HDRA's latest research into horticultural techniques that do not use chemicals.

Human Scale Education

96 Carlingcott, Nr. Bath, BA2 8AW, UK
Telephone or Fax: 01275 332516
E-mail: hse@clara.net
Web: www.hse.org.uk

Human Scale Education believes that small classes, small schools and larger schools restructured into smaller units are critical to providing the right kind of environment in which children can flourish. HSE tries to encourage larger schools to restructure and also supports home-based education and small school education projects. It encourages the democratic participation of children in their education and provides a welcome antidote to the homogenisation of education by central government.

Internet

There are dozens of web-sites dedicated to simple living. Many of them are, naturally enough, American. Some sites contain such sparkling gems as "If you need a new freezer, why not save money by buying one second-hand" – of course, this had never occurred to you, had it? A vast number of them are concerned with living frugally, such as Dollar Stretcher (www.stretcher.com) or Cheapskate Monthly (www.cheapskatemonthly.com). Some sites require you to subscribe to either a print or on-line magazine. Why pay for this, when you can glean most of the information free of charge?

One of the most useful sites is Frugal Corner at www.best.com/~piner/. It has links to many other sites that might be of interest to you.

Of course, if you have to buy a thousand pounds' worth of computer just to check all this out, you're already failing to think like a downshifter.

Letslink UK

12 Southcote Road, London, N19 5BJ, UK
Telephone: 020 7607 7852
Fax: 020 7609 7112
E-mail: lets@letslink.org
Web: www.letslink.org

LETS takes the idea of bartering goods and services and then moves it on a stage further. Instead of simply swapping directly with another individual, local people combine to form a club where they can trade goods and skills amongst themselves, using their own form of credit. Each club has a database of members and the skills, goods, items they are offering and a list of wants. My local LETS scheme has members offering anything from babysitting to counselling, willow baskets to tool hire. Wants are equally as wide-ranging, including horse riding lessons, patio laying, treatment for sciatica and free range eggs.

Mailing Preference Services

Freepost 22, London W1E 7EZ, UK
Telephone: 020 7766 4410

If you write to them, they will contact various companies which send unsolicited mail and ensure that your name and address are removed from their mailing lists.

The National Association of Citizens Advice Bureaux

Myddelton House, 115-123 Pentonville Road, London,
  N1 9LZ, UK
Telephone: 020 7833 2181
Fax: 020 7833 4371
Web: www.nacab.org.uk

Over five million people every year seek out the help of their local Citizens' Advice Bureau. The CAB is especially well-positioned to give advice on social security claims, employment rights, housing issues, legal problems, help with tax and a host of consumer problems. They are also renowned for their expertise in debt counselling and have been a life-line for countless people who are struggling to make ends meet. They offer free, confidential and impartial advice and information. If you don't need help, you could consider volunteering instead.

The Natural Medicines Society

PO Box 232, East Molesey, Surrey, KT8 1YF, UK
Telephone and Fax: 020 8974 1166
E-mail: nms@charity.vfree.com

NMS was set up in 1985 to represent freedom of choice in medicine. At a time when traditional and non-orthodox medicines were under attack from the medical establishment, the NMS helped in putting traditional medicine back on the map.

NMS campaigns for improved training standards for non-orthodox medical practitioners and complementary therapists, an increase in the number of natural medicines available and to make complementary and alternative medicine more widely available. They also want more research into the use of complementary medicine, in order to help put it on the same scientific footing as orthodox medicine.

Neighbourhood Initiatives Foundation

The Poplars, Lightmoor, Telford, TF4 3QN, UK
Telephone: 01952 590777
Fax: 01952 591771
E-mail: info@nif.co.uk
Web: www.nif.co.uk

The Neighbourhood Initiatives Foundation believes that communities can only really develop by encouraging people who live in them to develop a sense of responsibility for their own environments. NIF works with communities all over the UK, from Accrington to Ystalfera, to encourage participation, democracy and caring at local level. They work with local groups to improve housing estates, encourage local economic regeneration and to involve communities in the planning process.

The New Economics Foundation

Cinnamon House, 6-8 Cole Street, London, SE1 4YH, UK
Telephone: 020 7407 7447
Fax: 020 7407 6473
Email info@neweconomics.org
Web: www.neweconomics.org

"Money is only part of the whole economy," says the New Economics Foundation, a green think tank devoted to building a just and sustainable economy. NEF seeks to persuade commercial, public and not-for-profit organisations to balance their financial performance with social and environmental duties. They promote participation in the democratic process, encourage voluntary organisations to re-define what they want of society and are also at the heart of the movement for the introduction of community finance initiatives, such as LETS, community loans and social funds.

New Ways to Work

22 Northumberland Ave, London, WC2N 5AP, UK
Telephone: 020 7930 0093
Fax: 020 7930 3366
E-mail: info@new-ways.co.uk
Web: www.new-ways.co.uk

New Ways to Work state that their aim is to change the culture in the workplace to give real freedom of choice to individuals who cannot or do not wish to work traditional patterns. They advise on flexible working arrangements, which includes part-time work, job sharing, flexible working hours, term-time working, career breaks, sabbaticals and working from home. New Ways to Work deal with enquiries from both employers and employees, run training sessions and publish fact sheets and books. They also publish a newsletter to keep members up-to-date.

The Pedestrians' Association

31-33 Bondway, London, SW8 1SJ, UK
Telephone: 020 7820 1010
Fax: 020 7820 8208
E-mail: info@pedestrians.org.uk
Web: www.pedestrians.org.uk

The Pedestrians' Association works to make walking safer, easier and more convenient. They promote walking (as opposed to using the car) for short journeys and promote the rights and safety of people on foot. At local level, they campaign to have pedestrians rights on the agenda, for example when town centres are re-developed.

Permaculture Association

BCM Permaculture Assoc., London, WC1N 3XX, UK
Telephone: 07041 390 170
E-mail: office@permaculture.org.uk
Web: www.permaculture.org.uk

Permaculture is a contraction of "permanent agriculture, permanent culture". The concept is that people should design sustainable systems for living, drawing on traditional methods, the best of modern science and the ethics of caring for the earth. It helps people to work out their own solutions to local and global problems. Members receive a copy of the handbook, a quarterly newsletter and discounts on books and green services.

Positive News

No. 5 Bicton Enterprise Centre, Clun, Shropshire, SY7
    8NF, UK
Telephone: 01588 640 022
Fax: 01588 640 033
E-mail: office@positivenews.org.uk
Web: www.positivenews.org.uk

Positive News does exactly what its name suggests and prints positive news. Most of their stories are concerned with the environment, ecology, alternative power, organic lifestyles and general alternatives to orthodox living. It is available on subscription, but is often to be found free-of-charge at health food shops and the like. They also publish a sister magazine called "Living Lightly with Positive News", which carries slightly more in-depth articles.

Probono

1 The Warren, Handcross, West Sussex, RH17 6DX, UK
Telephone: 01444 400403
Fax: 01444 400493
E-mail: info@probono.org.uk

Probono's literature says, "Many are aware that the real quality of life depends not only on our income but on the quality of our relationships: with ourselves, one another, and our environment. We perceive the necessity to work without compromising our personal values, and we need and want to use our work to develop ourselves". Probono is a network of like-minded people in business and other professions who are looking to develop their businesses alongside personal growth. The idea is that Probono provides not just a forum for ideas, but also a means by which members promote their businesses and activities within the group.

Schumacher UK

The Create Environment Centre, Smeaton Road, Bristol,
BS1 6XN, UK
Telephone/Fax: 01179 031081
E-mail: schumacher@gn.apc.org
Web: www.oneworld.org/schumachersoc

The Society has sprung out of the work of the distinguished British economist E. F. Schumacher. His 1973 book *Small is Beautiful* pointed out many of the challenges that technology brings to modern life. He argued that materialism and the headlong rush towards increasingly large industries are a waste of resources. The Society carries the Schumacher message to the world with lectures, a mail-order book service, a newsletter and a series of annual awards for individuals and businesses "whose commitment and work gives hope and encouragement to others".

The Soil Association

Bristol House, 40-56 Victoria Street, Bristol, BS1 6BY, UK
Telephone: 01179 290661
Fax: 01179 252504
E-mail: info@soilassociation.org
Web: www.soilassociation.org

The Soil Association promotes and develops alternatives to intensive agriculture. They promote the use of organic farming methods and campaign against genetically-modified crops, intensive farming systems and the use of chemicals in farming. If you buy any product carrying the Soil Association logo, you can be assured that it conforms to the stringent "Standards for Organic Food and Farming" regulations.

In addition, the Association also believes that by promoting organic methods they are also encouraging a wider range of wildlife habitats, including more hedgerows and wider field margins.

Sustrans

PO Box 21, Bristol, BS99 2HA, UK
Telephone: 0117 9290888
Fax: 0117 9150124
E-mail: info@nationalcyclenetwork.org.uk
Web: www.sustrans.org.uk

Sustrans is short for "sustainable transport". They aim to reduce the amount of motor traffic on our roads by encouraging people to walk and cycle more. Sustrans' big project is the National Cycle Network that aims to connect together 8,000 miles of cycle routes. They aim to have half the network free from motor traffic by using old railway lines, canal towpaths and derelict land. Sustrans also promotes the idea of safe routes for schools – healthy, sociable, low-cost and non-polluting – with some free literature. They also sell a wide range of cycle maps.

TCA – The Telework, Telecottage and Telecentre Association

WREN Telecottage, Stoneleigh Park, Warwickshire,
    CV8 2RR, UK
Telephone: 024 76 696986
Fax: 024 76 696538

E-mail: tca@ruralnet.org.uk
Web: www.tca.org.uk

With over a million people in the United Kingdom doing some form of teleworking from home and the figures rising steadily each year, this is obviously an important area for the future. The TCA provides support and information for anyone involved in this kind of work. When you join the TCA you get a bi-monthly magazine, a weekly e-zine, a copy of their handbook (which gives information on teleworking, office equipment, training, health and safety, the legal aspects of teleworking and much more), access to other teleworkers, information and advice and TCA negotiates discounts on a number of products including home-business insurance.

Transport 2000

The Impact Centre, 12-18 Hoxton Street, London, N1
   6NG, UK
Telephone: 020 7613 0743
Fax: 020 7613 5280

Worried by the huge impact that the motorcar has on the environment and our everyday lives, Transport 2000 campaigns for measures that will cut down the number of vehicles on our roads and for improved public and alternative transport solutions. Among the initiatives they support are "the walking bus", a system whereby children walk to school, shepherded by adults, and "living streets", which aims to reduce traffic in urban areas and allow people to use the streets for a host of other activities, not just motoring.

Triodos Bank

Brunel House, 11 The Promenade, Clifton, Bristol, BS8
   3NN, UK

Telephone: 0500 008 720 (free)
Fax: 01179 739303
E-mail: mail@triodos.co.uk
Web: www.triodos.co.uk

Triodos Bank boasts that it is an ethical bank, lending only to businesses, charities and enterprises that are building a sustainable future. The bank invests in such businesses as organic farming, renewable energy, social housing and fair trade organisations. They offer a range of accounts for savers as well as accounts for charities and businesses.

The United Kingdom Co-operative Council

c/o The Co-operative Bank plc, PO Box 101, 1 Balloon
    Street, Manchester, M60 4EP, UK
Telephone: 0161 829 5290
Fax: 0161 832 9707

This is the umbrella organization for a variety of co-operatives working in the areas of agriculture, banking, community development, credit unions, housing, insurance and workers' co-operatives. Formed in 1991 by co-operative organisations, UKCC provides a forum for debate amongst a variety of co-operatives who together employ more than 140,000 people in the United Kingdom. They also publish a bi-annual magazine giving updates on activities in the co-operative sector.

Waste Watch

Europa House, Ground Floor, 13-17 Ironmonger Row,
    London, EC1V 3QG, UK
Telephone: 020 7253 6266
Fax: 020 7253 5962

E-mail: info@wastewatch.org.uk
Web: www. wastewatch.org.uk
General recycling enquiries – Waste Watch Wasteline:
   0870 243 0136

Waste Watch is a national charity aimed at promoting the reduction, reuse and recycling of waste. They publish a whole series of leaflets and books to help individuals, schools, communities and businesses combat waste. They also have an extremely informative website where you can find all sorts of useful information and ideas on waste reduction and reuse/recycling.

Willing Workers on Organic Farms

PO Box 2675, Lewes, East Sussex, BN7 1RB, UK
Web: www.wwoof.org

WWOOF works on an exchange basis. You get to stay on an organic farm, garden or smallholding, where you are given meals and accommodation and learn about organic growing methods. In exchange, you give your labour. WWOOF also has international links, which means that, for a fee, you can do the same thing in a number of other countries.

Workers' Educational Association

Temple House, 17 Victoria Park Square, London, E2 9PB,
   UK
Telephone: 020 8983 1515
Fax: 020 8983 4840
E-mail: info@wea.org.uk
Web: www.wea.org.uk

The WEA is a long-established organisation that provides

adult education throughout the United Kingdom. Over 140,000 students enrol on the thousands of courses that they hold in village halls, schools, colleges and community centres throughout the country. Their central idea that education should be a democratic process is reflected in the way in which local branches (of which there are 650) organise their own courses.

Work-Life Balance

Telephone: 020 7492 4280
E-mail: team.work-life-balance@dfee.gov.uk
Web: www.dfee.gov.uk/work-lifebalance

This is a Department for Education and Employment Initiative designed to encourage companies to realise at long last that a balanced worker is a healthier worker and, thus, a better worker. They provide examples of people who have altered the balance of their work and companies that have encouraged employees to do so. They can also supply a list of good practice for employers and several examples of companies that have become more productive as a result of a change in their attitude to employees' working arrangements.

Index